Canine Reproduction and Whelping

A Dog Breeder's Guide

Myra Savant-Harris RN

Distributed by Dogwise Publishing

Dedication

It gives me great pleasure to dedicate this book to my lovely boy, AKC Champion Peakdowns Aidan. By watching Aidan and his fabulous little nose, which was followed by fabulous little puppies, I have gained an education that all the books in the world could not have given me.

AKC Champion Peakdowns Aidan

Acknowledgements

I would like to thank the following individuals for their work on this book:

Cover design: Joann Opel

Cover photographer: Caroline Baines

Photography: L. Calyn Miller

Editing: L. Calyn Miller and Eileen Starks

I greatly appreciate their hard work and encouragement. Without the help and technical assistance from my son, Calyn, I literally could not have completed this book, nor "Puppy Intensive Care".

Table of Contents

Introduction

How Did I Get Here?

Although I worked as a labor/delivery and neonatal ICU RN for many years and assisted in literally hundreds of human births, I was very intimidated by the process of whelping my first few litters of puppies. It was rather puzzling to me why delivering a human baby had become so routine to me while whelping a litter of puppies seemed so scary. I had some conversations with some other dog breeders who also happened to be either nurses or physicians, and we all shared the same fears. Although we were all careful and thoughtful about the jobs that we did, none of us faced our daily work with actual fear. But yet, as experienced as we were in our various fields of practice, not one was comfortable when it came to assisting our bitches in the delivery of their puppies. After thinking this through carefully, I came to a clear understanding of why delivering puppies was so much more daunting than assisting in the delivery of babies.

In human medicine, a health care provider becomes very dependent upon your patient to TELL you things. They walk into your department literally pouring out information. They verbalize everything. They can tell you when their contractions started, how they feel, where they hurt, how their last delivery went, how many babies they are carrying; even the gender. Once you get them settled, you are able to do a vaginal exam that enlightens you even further. The first two fingers on my right hand were highly educated. They could tell me all about effacement, dilatation, presentation, position and more. Those two fingers could even tell me if the baby had hair or not. They were my best friends. They gave me even more information than the mother could tell me. So a vaginal exam, coupled with a verbal history from the mother, gave me a great deal of information and with information and knowledge came confidence.

My bitches on the other hand could not verbalize anything to me. Sure, they could dig around in my closet, but for crying out loud, what was that supposed to tell me? It's not as thought they had never gotten in my closet and dug around before so what exact piece of information was I to gain from watching that behavior? I was told early on that to do a vaginal exam on a small dog I was supposed to use the little finger. The LITTLE finger? That is the stupid finger. It doesn't know anything. It can barely get the latex glove on without screwing up all the other fingers. Good grief. The little finger was the one that usually ended up taped to a wound or something, and it was my information source? Oh my. We were in so much trouble.

So let me get this straight… all I had was a non-verbal pregnant mom digging in the closet and my little finger? Where was my fetal monitor? Where was the OR team? Where were the Respiratory Therapists who came at the buzz of a call button? Where were my good dependable moms bursting with verbal information? ("I have to push. I have to push NOW.") Most of all… where were those cervixes, which kept me informed of the laboring process every step of the way. Clearly, I had a lot of adapting to do. My job was to learn about the canine birth process without the benefit of sophisticated technology, spoken language and lots of professional help at my fingertips.

It took me a while to figure out that the bitches had lots of information to give me. I had to learn how to correlate their behaviors and anatomical changes with the various stages of gestation and labor. My little finger, while admittedly not very well educated and still a tad on the ignorant side, could at least tell me if there was a puppy in the birth canal. Sometimes it could snag a placenta which had been left behind and get it out of the way. After several litters, I began to be able to put the pieces together and start to function as a canine labor/delivery RN. Books helped me, but I had to read several of them in order to learn the things I needed. Conversations with my repro specialist, Dr. Cindy helped immeasurably. Talking with other breeders who so graciously shared their experiences helped a lot. After my first book, "Puppy Intensive Care" began to do so well and I starting giving seminars on the book, I began to see the need for a second book. Breeders were asking me for a book about the canine reproductive system and how to whelp their puppies. After two years of research and dawdling… here it is. I am hopeful that my experience as a labor/delivery nurse, coupled with the many, many things I have read and researched, combined with the things that other dog fanciers have shared will result in a book that will assist breeders. I have tried to make it easy to read, easy to understand and educational in all ways.

As I have written the book, I have been acutely aware that for some of you, parts of it may be too simplistic, while for others, it will be filled with new information. My hope is that each reader will take away something from this book that will make a positive difference in your careers as dog breeders.

1- To Breed or Not to Breed
Breeding is About Both Ethics and Genetics

Actually, it may be a question, but you won't find an answer from me; pointers maybe—perhaps even a suggestion or two, but answers… no. Obviously, I have opinions; I am a dog breeder after all. I have a personal philosophy of breeding and things that I hope to accomplish with each breeding. I believe in health testing. There may be a book out there about breeding and personal ethics, but this book is not it. This book is about canine reproduction and whelping…but personal ethics are part of that picture.

My goal is to teach you the things that you need to know in order to breed your dogs and help your bitches to whelp their litters—plain and simple. My goal is to teach, not to preach; and if everything works out the way it should, that is all that will happen within these pages. With any luck at all, my soapbox will remain in its corner (well, most of the time anyhow).

Now, having said that, I would like to have you consider all of the ramifications of breeding your dogs. Just considering all of the factors involved may help you come to a well-thought out, valid decision before the sperm has said "howdy" to the egg, so to speak.

Sometimes It's About Ethics

Before you make a decision to breed your dogs, decide what it is you hope to accomplish. What is your goal, other than to have a litter of puppies? Do you want to better the breed? Do you want to win in the show ring with something that you have produced yourself instead of purchased? Do you want to work on specific health issues that could be decreased or maybe even eliminated with careful breeding practices? Do you want to provide little Susie and little Bobby with an opportunity to witness the "miracle of birth"? (Please just say no.) Are you hoping to finance that long-awaited trip to Hawaii? (Again, just say no.) What are your goals? Put them in writing.

If providing your kids with an education that involves the miracle of birth is your goal…forget it. If a puppy buyer asks for breeding privileges so that their kids can enjoy a litter of puppies, or so that they can recoup their investment, think it over carefully before you let them walk out the door with one of your puppies. First, what they may end up providing themselves with is an expensive stud fee and a breeding that doesn't take in the first place. Second, you may be providing them with an education about c-sections in the middle of the night, and puppies may be dying right and left because they don't know what they are doing. Worst of all, Sue and Bob may end up being the kids sitting in front of the grocery store with a litter of puppies in a cardboard box willing to pawn them off on the first warm body to say yes to a puppy. Does anyone need an education like this?

Before you allow "Stud Muffin" to impregnate "In-Season Sadie", keep in mind that humane societies all over the United States are putting thousands of dogs to death every week. These are dogs that simply weren't wanted by anyone. Oh, someone may have wanted them when they were adorable little pups sitting in a box outside of the grocery store (heaven forbid) or advertised in the newspaper, (not all that great either) but when push came to shove… these were dogs who simply were not loved, and were not valued and treasured. Someone made a conscious decision to breed those dogs, or they carelessly allowed the dogs to take matters into their own paws because of their failure to spay and neuter. Do you want to produce puppies that will end up being killed because they are not wanted? Do you want to produce puppies that will end up as adults tied to trees in the yard, ignored except for a daily feeding and watering? Large numbers of puppies who are born live horrible lives and meet a quick demise at the hands of owners who have tired of them. Consider these factors *before* you do a breeding, not while the Doberman Pincher from next door is tied with your little Cocker Spaniel girl and your fence is lying in pieces in your back yard. A lot of dog breeding simply should not be taking place. Good breeders, however, are working hard to address the longevity and quality of life of dogs.

Conscientious, careful breeders are producing thousands of puppies every year, each of whom will be lovingly and carefully placed into wonderful homes to provide years of pleasure and companionship to carefully chosen owners. Good breeders are making good breeding choices, such as:

- Never breeding more pups than can be placed in good homes.
- Never breeding a dog that is affected by a known genetically transmitted disease.
- Taking back their pups for re-homing if the need arises.
- Religiously testing their dogs for diseases prevalent within their breed.
- Not placing pups in pet stores for selling.
- Placing pet quality animals with spay and neuter contracts.
- Mentoring new puppy buyers and breeders thoughtfully and patiently.

Sometimes It's About Genetics

This is a good place to address the genetic "carrier status" of our dogs. Because we keep good records and our puppies' buyers feel free to call us with problems, over time, we begin to develop a database of the flaws our dogs are carrying. Carrier status means that genetically, our dog carries the gene for a flaw or defect without exhibiting the defect and without being affected. We may be producing the occasional monorchid (one testicle), the occasional slipping patellae, even the occasional more serious congenital or acquired defect in our puppies. Many of these flaws/defects are genetic in nature.

Books on canine genetics do not recommend that we discard a dog with carrier status from our breeding programs, particularly if the dog has a great deal to offer the breed. Geneticists tell us that we breed away from the genetic flaw. We look for mates who have not been producers of the defect. If you have a bitch who has produced two dog pups with one testicle and a couple with luxating patellae, your job is to put some real effort into finding a boy who has not been producing those problems. Stud dog owners need to practice good disclosure policies. In the long-run, it will enhance your reputation within the breed. Other breeders will admire your honesty and you have a chance to set an example.

Brutality and SNP

Another way that we can become better breeders is to be brutal in our breeding programs, and I do mean... brutal. No matter how much you love a specific dog, if the dog is producing bad temperaments, spay/neuter and place. If your dog is diagnosed with a genetically transmitted disease... SNP. If your dog, although a multiple BIS winner, consistently produces pets... SNP. The magic bullet in a breeding program that grows and gets better over time is this: SNP. Spay Neuter and Place. If you cannot bear to part with the dog... fine. Then just SN. However, unless you have unlimited space and energy, you will soon be caring for, feeding and housing a kennel filled with dogs who can't be used for breeding. SNP. Breeding is all about improvement. If a dog is not able to create pups that represent an improvement... Spay Neuter and Place. The improvement doesn't have to be huge; it just has to represent an improvement over what you already have in your kennel or what you have produced in the past. Being brutal takes a huge emotional toll on you. Are you willing to pay it?

Sometimes It's About Prepotency

You can afford to be somewhat forgiving with a bitch. She isn't going to produce hundreds of puppies in her lifetime. She will produce very few compared to what a heavily used and well-loved stud dog will sire. A female, however is also considered to be prepotent and can often contribute her genetic load and stamp her get in the same way that a dog can, she simply cannot do it as many times. For that reason, a prepotent stud dog, the dog with the power and dominant genes necessary to imprint his hereditary characteristics on his pups, has a value far beyond money. He has the capability to bring about permanent change in the breed—even in the species.

For many generations, horse breeders believed that only stallions were prepotent: capable of stamping their get with their desirable qualities. The general perception was that broodmares were simply incubators. It was not until the famous Man o' War came along that breeders understood that mares too were prepotent and that their genetic characteristics could override those of the stallion. Man o' War's sire, Fair Play, was a diminutive little racer who never won a race. Fair Play's sire was a horse named Hastings, who was famous for biting any horse who tried to pass him on the track... Man o' War's dam, Mahubah, however, was a giant. From his mother, Man o' War inherited a thirty-foot stride, a cannon bone an inch longer than the average, a chest five inches broader, and a gentle disposition. All that Man o'War inherited from his sire was the habit of chewing on his hooves, in the same way that people bite their fingernails. Mares and bitches alike are also prepotent.

What is a "Sport"?

Sport is not a very commonly used term in dog breeding. It is common in reference to the genetics behind gardening and botany, but we hear it used much less in reference to canine breeding and genetics. A 'sport' is a dog that, although he has fabulous qualities, is unable to produce them in his get. He is unable to reproduce himself. We have all seen sports. We have all heard about them. We often see them winning like mad in the show ring…but we never see their off spring following along in their footsteps. How is a "sport" created? Who the heck knows? We can only speculate. Have you ever seen a litter of mediocre pups with one truly outstanding example of the breed nestled in the whelping nest? Chances are good that this puppy will be a "sport". He may be a ribbon-winning fool, but he may not be able to reproduce himself. Why is this so? It is because he is the genetic inconsistency in the litter. He is the single example of quality in an otherwise unremarkable litter. Like the botanical equivalent, when bred this dog may in all likelihood, revert to genetic mediocrity. On the other hand, have you ever seen a litter in which every single puppy finished as champions? Better to have gotten third pick of that litter than first pick of the litter with one sparkling example of the breed. When choosing a puppy for showing and breeding, look for consistency. Search for consistency in the parents, the grandparents, and most of all… the littermates. Genetic consistency is the key to successful dog breeding.

Dog breeders are also, in a way, creators of life. There are responsibilities that go along with the creation of each of those little lives no matter how you view it. Please take the responsibilities of canine breeding seriously. Be one of those breeders who makes good choices and tries with every breeding to better your breed. Make sure that the footprint that you leave behind in your breed is a footprint heading into the right direction.

2- Different Strokes For Different Species

Misconceptions About Conception: "They" Is Not "Us"

Even though Fifi seems like your daughter and Fido feels like the son you never had, there are real and fundamental differences between the canine species and human beings. Sometimes the differences are refreshing. For example, every time Fifi gets pregnant, you get to pick the boyfriend and sell the grandkids that you don't wish to keep, and when Fido fathers children from one end of the country to the other, both you and he are building a positive reputation, and you get paid to boot. Woo hoo! Try that with a human son. However, it is the desire to "humanize" our dogs that sometimes leads to misconceptions, misunderstandings, and even missed breedings and terrified trips to the vet.

In order to understand the process of breeding and whelping your dogs, you must first have a clear concept of how we differ from them. Truly, 'they' is not 'us'. This chapter is about some of the misconceptions that can create confusion about breeding and whelping. Canines are anatomically different, hormonally different, and their motivation for breeding is different as well. Contrary to what many people think, breeding activities are not recreational to a dog. They breed to create life and reproduce themselves. They chew on a chewy and chase a ball to have fun.

Only the human mammal views reproduction as an entertaining and bonding experience. Very few mammals are equipped for sexual activity round the clock. Though men and women are able to enjoy sexual activity at all times, the woman is only fertile for 2-3 days per month. Dogs are geared to reproduce not to have fun or bond with a spouse. A bitch comes into season approximately twice a year, sometimes less; and at all other times, she has no interest in breeding activities.

A young pup may attempt to have a sexually meaningful relationship with his stuffed toys, but once he has been bred, he quickly learns the difference between a bitch and a Teddy Bear. You will notice that you can easily leave an intact dog and an intact bitch together at all times until she comes in season. An experienced stud dog will not mount a bitch that is not in season. A truly experienced and knowledgeable stud dog will not even mount a bitch that is in season until her eggs are down. If his nose is really, really good and there isn't any competition for the bitch, he won't attempt breeding until his nose tells him that the eggs are ripe and ready. If his nose tells him that the eggs have already been fertilized, he may not want to touch the bitch at all. If the bitch "feels" that her eggs have been fertilized, she may well refuse the dog as well. If you remember that the act of copulation is, for all dogs, only about reproduction and not about "fun", you will better understand canine behaviors when it comes to breeding. To put it another way: it is not about libido, it is all about knowledge; and their little noses give them a lot of information that only they can know.

If your stud dog is a little bit slow on the draw and you would like to get him jump-started, bring another intact boy into the picture and that will often get things going. Even if his nose tells him that the timing isn't perfect, he won't want to take the chance that the other intact boy will take the opportunity to reproduce. He may well do a breeding even when his nose tells him the timing is not perfect. Competition to see who gets to pass on their genetics to the next generation can tip the scales a little bit in your favor. So let's get started on some of the basic differences between "us" and "them". In the space allotted, I can only point a few of the differences, but they will be key to understanding canine reproduction and whelping.

We can begin with the word "erection". A man must be fully erect before he can penetrate a woman. On the other hand, once the dog is fully erect, he has missed his window of opportunity for penetration. His penis is constructed differently. The dog's penis is erect at all times. It is small and tucked away into the sheath of skin that contains it, but is constructed of firm cartilage that is anatomically placed at the right angle to penetrate the bitch. It is narrow, short and firm, with a relatively small bulb near the body. Once he is in the vagina of the bitch, his penis becomes significantly longer, wider and the bulb at the point closest to his body enlarges from the size of a large marble (on a toy breed) to a good sized plum or small apple. It is the swelling of the bulb that keeps the penis in place inside the bitch long enough for him to ejaculate the full three fractions of his ejaculation. The common term for this is a "tie". The scientific term is copulatory lock.

If you have been trying to get your dog and your bitch to breed, and he is dragging his penis around on the floor, you are finished with that breeding for the time being. Once the dog is fully erect, it is too late for him to penetrate the bitch. You will need to put him away alone by himself in a crate for a while to get back down to normal size and then try again later. Understanding this will help you to know how to assist inexperienced stud dogs to achieve their goal. He needs to enter the vagina while he is still relatively small, and thrust a few times while he becomes engorged. By the time those things have happened, he has become erect, the bulb has enlarged significantly and he cannot release himself from the bitch until the size of the bulb reduces. His natural instinct will be to lift one of his rear legs over the tie and they may end up rear end to rear end. As they relax, they may even lay side by side. His penis is quite elastic in nature and he or she may lay down during the tie. A tie may last from 5 minutes to an hour or so. Everything that needs to happen has probably happened within the first 5-10

6

minutes. If you are getting bored with the lengthy ties, a good trick is to offer each of them a peanut butter spoon. They become distracted eating the peanut butter and soon the tie is over.

Obviously, the timing for canines is all off when compared to human beings. It differs from dog breed to dog breed, but in most breeds, the bitches come into season only once or twice per year. Women, on the other hand, "come into season" once every 28 days. One of their ovaries usually releases a single egg that lives only 24 hours, although as in all mammals, the sperm has a longer lifespan. Although studies have shown that their hormone status may increase the sexual drive of a female human, it is nothing when compared to the sexual drive of a bitch in heat.

A bitch in season will mount other bitches, allow other bitches to mount her and display outrageously flirtatious behavior toward the males. One of their favorite tricks is to turn with their rear end facing the dog, with a little flirtatious look on their faces. Sometimes a bitch will back her rear end into the dogs' face while flagging her tail energetically. She may "Butt Bopp" him as soon as her eggs are released, but he may wait and save his energy and his sperm for the time when the eggs are actually going to be ripe and receptive to the sperm. Remember, it is not about <u>recreation</u> to the dog—it is about <u>reproducing</u> himself. That is what drives his sexual behaviors.

The eggs that the bitch releases will live approximately four to five days. Their bodies are designed to carry, develop and feed multiples. When the eggs are released, they are in a primary or immature state, needing two-three full days to develop or ripen. Once ripe, they live another two days. In most cases, the bitch is highly motivated to be bred although she may not have the necessary experience to know exactly how to go about it. She may keep looking over her shoulder to see what the heck is going on and every time she does, he will lose his aim. You may need to hold her at those times. Some bitches will never be receptive to a dog and when this happens, you will have to make hard decisions about whether or not you want to leave her in your breeding program. There is always artificial insemination for those bitches who are not receptive to a dog if you decide that her other good qualities outweigh this undesirable one.

You will more commonly see a timing issue versus an across-the-board rejection of all males. There are a couple of things you can check on the bitch to evaluate her timing. If you lightly stroke the vulva of a bitch that has ripe eggs, the vulva will lift slightly. Her tail should shift over to the side to uncover the vulva. That would allow the penis to reach the vulva for breeding. That particular behavior is called "flagging". If you stroke the vulva with a gloved finger and place the finger slightly inside of the vulva, you can often feel a clasping movement. These involuntary movements of the bitch can signify to you that the timing for a breeding is good. If her body is doing these involuntary things but she is still rejecting the male, you will want to consider artificial insemination.

Once the eggs have either been fertilized, or have died, some stud dogs may still have an interest in her, particularly the younger, less experienced boys. They are interested in the odors that she still carries. As she comes out of her season, she will quickly let them know that she no longer welcomes their advances. Keep her separated from them to keep her from being molested, and give her a complete bath and grooming before she is allowed back into your general population of dogs. Watch her carefully when you reintroduce her into the group. Protect her from the advances of the boys who may not yet fully understand that she can no longer be bred.

Although we would never dream of preparing our sons for breeding activities, we should prepare our young dogs from puppy hood. A young dog who is allowed to run with the older boys who have been used for breeding purposes will usually be considered a non-dominant dog. The dominant, or alpha, dog may well feel that all breeding is to be done by him. All the bitches belong to him. If this is his thought process, he will often harass the younger boys to keep them submissive. He will growl at them and put them down on their backs in order to enforce his dominance over them. Some dogs try to set up a little social order similar to that of wolves in which only the alpha dog does the breeding. If you have a young boy that you intend to use for breeding, you should probably be taking steps to protect him from the alpha behaviors of your dominant stud dog. You should also be introducing him briefly, and away from the other stud dogs, to bitches in season. From early puppy hood, expose him to the girls who are in early season or late season so that he too, can begin to develop his "nose" without being harassed by the other dogs in your kennel. Give him an opportunity to be in the presence of girls who are of breeding age. Watch him carefully when you do this because you certainly don't want an accidental breeding at seven months of age. If he acts interested in the girl, praise him. Many breeders who have allowed their male pup to run freely with their stud dogs wonder why the younger dog is reluctant to complete a breeding when he is given the opportunity. Often it is because he has learned that he is submissive to the alpha dog and is not supposed to be the breeding animal. Make sure that you reinforce by your behaviors, the idea that he is a future stud dog.

If you do artificial inseminations in your kennel, you will also need to prepare your young boys for the collection process. From the time they are young pups, put them on a counter (toys and medium sized dogs can easily be trained to collect on a counter top covered by a non-skid rug) and gently stroke their prepuce until you begin to feel it getting erect. Give them praise and a cookie and let them be on their way. Once they are about a year old, collect them using an experienced girl who is in season and ready for breeding. Do this out of the sight of your older dogs. You may not use the semen, but you can still begin his training for collection of his sperm using an experienced girl who will not turn on him and scare him off the breeding game forever. Put it under a microscope and it you will have a chance to check it.

Green… Sometimes Scary, Sometimes Normal

There are some important differences in the overall whelping picture that should be crystal clear to a breeder. One of the most important whelping differences between humans and canines involves the color <u>green</u>. In human obstetrics, the color green during the birth process is a sign of genuine fetal distress. Almost every one who has had a human child has heard the term: meconium. Meconium is green and is always a bad sign prior to delivery. When the bag of waters ruptures in a human delivery and is green, or even very lightly green tinged, it is a sign of impending or past danger to the human fetus. In the whelping process, green is normal and natural. This is one more proof that "they" isn't "us". This is how they differ:

<u>Green is always bad in a human delivery</u>.

If the human fetus has a marked decrease in oxygen to his brain, he will lose consciousness. No one knows how long he may be unconscious, but we know that <u>any</u> loss of consciousness in the fetus is due to a lack of oxygen to the brain and this is never a good sign… never a good thing…always bad. If a human fetus loses consciousness while in utero, the sphincter muscle of the rectum will relax and open, releasing the contents of the large intestine into the amniotic fluid. The content of the large intestine is called meconium. Meconium is green in color and is a sign of fetal distress. Once the baby is born, it is very important that meconium is not aspirated into the lungs. In human deliveries, green is always a bad sign.

<u>Green is (most often) completely normal in a canine delivery</u>.

A portion of the canine placenta contains a green pigment. This green pigment is called uteroverdine. When it appears at the vulva, it is a sign of placental separation. It is a signal that a puppy is being born. It is not a bad sign. It is not a sign of fetal distress. It is normal for the color green to appear in the amniotic fluid of the puppy. If a placenta has been held back in the body of the bitch, the uteroverdine may even discolor a subsequent puppy slightly and the body of the puppy may be slightly green. This is not abnormal. Under almost all circumstances in the dog, green is not a bad sign. The amniotic sac may be quite green in a whelping situation and it is completely normal. The green is simply a by-product of the uteroverdine in the placenta. The canine placenta is also a very different organ than the human placenta. When a pup is born, it is impossible to see its actual shape, but the placenta for a puppy is like a belt. It encircles the entire puppy's body with the green part turned inward. The placenta attaches all the way around inside the uterine horn. During the first stage of labor is probably the time that the puppy slips out of

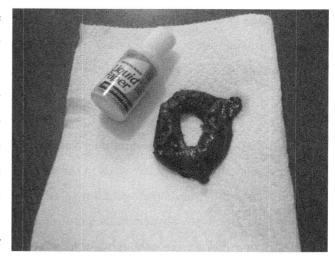

the "belt" leaving the placenta still attached to the uterine horn until shortly before birth. I've included a little bottle of white out so that you could see the size comparison of the placenta from a cavalier in the picture. The puppy is attached to his placenta by his umbilical cord. Human placentas are large pieces of tissue that are connected to the interior of the uterus and connected to the baby by the umbilical cord, but the placenta does not encircle the baby as it does a puppy. Human placentas do not have uteroverdine.

There is one exception. Because seeing green at the opening of the vulva is a signal that a puppy has separated from the placenta, it IS a bad sign if there is green, pasty looking discharge from the vulva and your bitch is not in labor. If your pregnant bitch is just walking around normally and is not in labor, green discharge means that a puppy has separated from the placenta and there are problems. Call your vet immediately.

False Pregnancy

One of the things that I found when writing this book is that sometimes I can't find the exact place that I want to put things. I decided to talk about "false pregnancy" under this section because it is also one of the things that are fairly common with bitches that humans do not experience. A false pregnancy, if you think about it, isn't really a false pregnancy at all. The pregnant bitch doesn't do much of anything except get a bigger tummy while they are gestating. It is only when they are getting ready to deliver that they get milk, begin nesting and start looking for little stuffed animals to nurture. These aren't pregnancy behaviors; they are whelping behaviors. A false pregnancy is caused by a decrease in progesterone levels in the same way that the whelping process begins with a decrease in progesterone levels. It is pretty common in the canine and not a cause for worry. Give your bitch time to get over it, watch her carefully and if she hasn't gotten through it in a week or so, contact your vet. Just remember that it is associated not with a breeding... but with a decrease in progesterone. It isn't associated with any of diseases associated with whelping or pregnancy.

In summary, our dogs are not us. They are not human. They are dogs and dogs function differently than humans do. Being aware of these essential differences will make the understanding of canine reproduction processes much easier.

Notes:

3- Sperm

Virility: Strength in Numbers

Before we start our discussion of sperm, we need to clarify two terms: semen and sperm. The term "semen" refers to the entire ejaculate, which contains both sperm and prostatic fluid. The word "sperm" refers only to the small DNA-carrying "swimmers" which will actually swim up stream to the egg and penetrate the egg, thus completing the fertilization.

Unlike the bitch, which is born with all the eggs (ovum) she will ever possess, neatly tucked away in her ovaries, dogs are born with two little manufacturing plants (testes) that keep pumping out sperm pretty much until the end of life. The prostate gland is the organ responsible for creating the fluid in which sperm is transported.

The number of eggs that the ovaries contain versus the number of sperm that the testes will produce over a lifetime is a perfect example of "overkill". This is an understatement to say the least. To give an example, while a human female ovulates a single egg every twenty-eight days, the human male will donate 40 million sperm per ejaculate in order to get that single egg fertilized.

A toy dog such as a Yorkshire terrier, will ejaculate somewhere in the neighborhood of 300-400 million sperm per ejaculate to fertilize the 2-6 eggs that a toy bitch might normally produce in a season. Indeed, he can ejaculate those 300-400 million sperm every day for 5 days without a noticeable loss of semen quality or libido. Studies have shown that if a dog is collected daily for 10-12 weeks, there will finally be a loss of libido. Sperm quality and quantity will begin to decline after 5-7 days of daily collections. However, even one hour after an ejaculation, the dog can be collected again and will produce 70-80% of the sperm in the first ejaculation. Seventy percent of 400 million is still quite a significant number. This is good news for the stud dog owner. Generally speaking, the stud dog, while responsible for the gender of the puppies, is not responsible for the size of the litter; not when he is ejaculating anywhere from approximately 300-400 million in the toy breeds to over one billion sperm at a time in the larger breeds.

Why, we ask ourselves, does it require 400 million sperm to fertilize say... 4 eggs? Well, the answer is that while sperm are indeed, determined and driven, they are also easily distracted by objects other than an egg and susceptible to annihilation by almost everything. Just about anything will kill sperm. A temperature increase in the testes of a couple of degrees over normal body temperature lasting 2-3 minutes will kill sperm in the testes. It won't kill the manufacturing plants in the testes, but it will surely kill the sperm that are already there. Sperm will regenerate but it might take six weeks or so for sperm producing abilities to be at full capacity. Repeating the insult to the testicles over time can cause permanent sterility. A lot of top show dogs have been blown dry into sterility.

What might cause this increase in temperature? Occasionally, a fever in the dog such as the type caused by illness or infection. Usually the body has protective methods by which it attempts to save the sperm. If a dog has a fever, the body's natural inclination will be to drop the testicles as far from the heat source as possible. This happens on a hot day as well. As the body heats up, the testicles will hang lower and lower in an attempt to remove themselves from the body and cool themselves off, thereby preserving the reproductive abilities of the sperm.

A good hot tub bath on show day will certainly cause that brief increase in body temperature, and so will the heat from blow-drying the rear end of your dog if you do not shield the testicles from the hot air. One good show weekend, with a couple of good hot baths and two nice long episodes of blow drying the rear end, and you might be wondering why your boy missed when bred to his last two bitches. He might have come home with a nice big blue ribbon, but he left his sperm at the fairgrounds. Heat will kill sperm. Keep the bath water tepid and use your hand to hold the testicles while directing the blow dryer away from the testicles for grooming.

Water will kill sperm. Our body fluids are saline (salt) based. Salt attracts water. If there is water inside of the syringe used for insemination or inside the insemination tube… even a drop, it will upset the saline/water content of the sperm. Water will be pulled into the sperm cells and the cells will explode. Even if you use water to rinse the vulva of the bitch prior to breeding, some of the sperm will die upon contact with the water from that little bath. Avoid water during the breeding process. Use a normal saline solution (I'll give you a recipe to make your own later in the book) to clean and rinse your insemination equipment and avoid the use of water on the vulva or penis at the time of breeding. Lubricants such as K-Y Jelly® will kill sperm. It is water based. Sure, people have used it forever, but whenever sperm came into contact with it, they died. Plain and simple. Water and any water-based lubricants will kill sperm.

Latex will kill sperm. Studies have shown that touching a collection of sperm with a latex glove will cause the demise of sperm. Certainly using a soft latex catheter to do an artificial insemination will cause the death of thousands of sperm. Be sure that the collection and insemination equipment you use is latex free. This is actually easy to do since so many people have developed allergies to latex. Most syringe boxes will say if the syringes are latex free. Read labels and avoid the use of latex containing products for sperm collection or storage. Use a silicone or plastic container to collect the sperm. The wide mouthed Playtex® baby bottle inserts work very well for most breeds of dogs. They are inexpensive, widely available and clean.

Detergents, soaps and bleach will kill sperm. Certainly, you are going to keeps things as clean as possible but for the cleaning of the equipment used for sperm collection and insemination, use very hot water to rinse it clean and then follow that with a complete rinsing of the equipment with normal saline. Place your equipment on a clean paper towel in a sunny windowsill to air dry and the sun will also do a good job of killing any microorganisms that might be on the equipment. For a certainty, all cleaning products will kill sperm. They might die clean... but die they will. They should probably all be stamped: "fragile". Of course, the stamping will kill them too, so it is up to you to understand that sperm is very fragile stuff.

We can be grateful that sperm is very, very determined in its effort to swim up stream, find a large round smooth object and penetrate it. The bad news is that sperm will attempt to penetrate just about any large, round, smooth object that they find on the way to the eggs. If you put a tiny drop of sperm on a slide, you can watch as thousands of them try to penetrate an air bubble. They are determined to penetrate that large, round, smooth object. They do not appear to be as attracted to angular, rougher shapes. How many millions of sperm get distracted on the way up stream toward the fallopian tubes (where all fertilization takes place) and spend their lifespan trying to penetrate a random red blood cell, or a nicely rounded piece of smooth cellular debris? How many take a wrong turn and end up in a small fold of vaginal tissue? My guess is millions and millions. That is why the overkill and the incongruent numbers: 2-6 eggs waiting patiently for the 2-6 sperm out of the original millions or even billion plus which were ejaculated. Sperm are indeed determined, but since it takes millions to get the job done, we can also assume they are easily distracted along the way. It truly is a wonder we have dogs at all.

A puppy dog will begin to manufacture sperm at some point between seven months and one year of age. By the time he is six or seven years of age, his sperm quality and quantity has decreased somewhat but he can still produce puppies until at least ten years and sometimes older. He is at his prime between eighteen months and six years of age. Very young dogs and very old dogs have poor sperm quality.

The amount of semen ejaculated during a single ejaculation varies between 1 and 75 ccs. Remember: semen is the entire ejaculate and contains the prostatic fluid. The amount of semen is size-related so toy dogs will produce less semen than larger breeds. The amount of sperm fraction is also size related so that toys have less quantity of sperm fraction per ejaculate than giant breeds. The actual sperm that is ejaculated ranges between one and six ccs. A three pound yorkie may only ejaculate 2 ccs of semen, with 1 cc being sperm and the other being prostatic fluid while a Great Dane may ejaculate 70 ccs or so of semen with only 6 ccs being sperm and the rest prostatic fluid. I can't find a reference that says this, but I suspect that the amount of sperm/semen ejaculated is pretty well adjusted to the distance that the sperm must travel to meet the targets. Yorkies do not need as much because the sperm don't have to swim as far to reach the eggs. Great Danes need more in order to insure that enough of them can make that longer journey to reach the eggs. That is just my little theory, based on nothing at all but conjecture. In addition, those breeds of dogs that are very large and have larger litters also have males who ejaculate greater numbers of sperm. More eggs necessitate more sperm.

Here is a rough breakdown of sperm production in milliliters/cubic centimeters (they're interchangeable). This is sperm only, not prostatic fluid, and these numbers represent averages. Sure, your dog may produce more... but there is no reason to celebrate or give him a cookie; it's a size related function, not a macho related function.

Body Weight and Sperm Quantity

10-34 pounds.........sperm content per ejaculation: 2.5 cc

35-40 pounds.........sperm content per ejaculation: 4.0 cc

50-60 pounds.........sperm content per ejaculation: 5.0 cc

60-84 pounds.........sperm content per ejaculation: 6.0 cc

The number of sperm for those sizes is somewhere between 300-400 million on the small dog end to approximately 1.5 billion on the large dog end. There are three fractions in every ejaculation. The first fraction is probably prostatic fluid. It is clear and very minimal, perhaps a few drops. This fraction is ejaculated during the really hard thrusting stages. The second fraction is the sperm rich fraction and is ejaculated near the end of the thrusting stage and at the very beginning of the tie stage. These first two fractions do not appear to have any sort of force behind them. They just drip out. The third fraction is the prostatic fluid and is ejaculated during the remainder of the tie. This fraction is ejected during a rhythmic pulsation of the penile tissue, particular the part behind the bulb. For a natural breeding, you will get and use all three fractions. For collection for chilling or freezing or artificial insemination, however, you will not need nor want the third fraction. Once the thrusting has stopped, allow 3-4 pulsations and then stop the collection process. The remainder of the ejaculate is superfluous fluid and not useful. Prostatic fluid does not make a suitable extender for chilled sperm and is, in fact, rather toxic to sperm. (Remember what I told you before... almost everything kills sperm, including prostatic fluid.) In fact, the difference between a collection with only sperm and prostatic fluid viewed under a microscope versus a collection which has been spun and cleaned of prostatic fluid and replaced by extender is quite dramatic. The sperm are livelier and definitely appear to be of a higher quality when they are extended.

 The acidity of the body fluids inside the bitch neutralize the prostatic fluid after it is ejaculated so that, while in a test tube it is rather toxic to sperm; inside the bitch it is neutralized and harmless. Because of the pulsating action, the purpose of the third fraction could be to propel the sperm rich fraction upward to speed it on the journey toward the eggs. Again, just conjecture on my part, no basis in actual fact.

If you collect sperm intended for insemination, it is always necessary to put it under a microscope to check to see if it is alive before you use it. A collection with dead sperm will still appear cloudy. With only a microscope and glass slides, you cannot do an actual sperm count, but at least you can visualize the sperm to see if they are alive and if the majority of them appear to be normal, active and moving in somewhat the same direction. If you see clumps of them trying to enter an air bubble, this is a good sign. They may not be very discerning, but at least they appear to know what to do with an egg should they happen upon one in their journeys. Roughly, 80% of the sperm in any one ejaculate are normal. The other 20% will have abnormalities of some sort: headless, tailless, two heads, seriously twisted or coiled tails, etc. This is also normal. Don't worry about it. No dog will produce sperm that is 100% perfect. Normal is the ratio of 80% normal, 20% abnormal.

Some stud dogs produce semen which contains sperm with large numbers of malformations such as proximal drops (small droplet looking objects behind the head of the sperm), funny looking tails or other little abnormalities. Much of this sperm is suitable for immediate insemination. It can't be chilled or frozen, but used fresh, the sperm can still get the job done and the DNA they carry is normal. Some flaws on sperm are not compatible with chilling or freezing, but the sperm is still useful and can produce puppies. Prior to using the dog at public stud, a good repro vet should evaluate your dogs' sperm and tell you about the quality, the quantity and any abnormalities that are there. All canine sperm is the same size, miniature poodle or Irish wolfhound, the sperm is the exact same size. The quantity will vary according to the size of the dog, but the size of the sperm is the same for all canines.

Evaluate the color of the semen prior to use:

Cloudy white………….Normal, healthy semen

Yellow……………….Contaminated with urine/purulent exudates

Green…………………Contaminated with purulent exudates

Red/Pink……………...Contaminated with fresh blood

Brown………………...Contaminated with old blood

Clear……………........No sperm present

If you collect your dog and the semen is clear with no sperm, do not panic immediately, but do get prepared to panic. Perhaps the dog was not feeling well, or you might not have given him a teaser bitch or a bitch he liked. There are things that can cause an ejaculation without sperm. If, however, you have collected only clear fluid for three collections in a row spaced out over six weeks or so, chances are very, very good that your dog is sterile and there is very little that can be done to fix it. If sperm count is low, or if the sperm are dead, some medical tests and remedies are well worth trying. Many repro vets recommend the use of Glycoflex (available through Drs Foster and Smith) to increase the quality and quantity of sperm. Use 300 mgs in the AM and again in the PM and after 90 days, you may way find that the numbers and quality of sperm have increased. Your repro specialist can guide and direct you through that process; but if the dog has no sperm at all, try to get used to the idea that he is sterile and it is permanent. There are two primary reasons for sterility in a dog. The first is that an infection of some sort caused the very delicate tubules to scar over and close. The infection could have been close to the testicles, such as the prostate gland, or it could have been farther away such as persistent dental infections. Blocked tubules cannot be fixed. Don't even ask; the answer is no.

Secondly, an internal injury to the testicle can cause internal bleeding and the dogs' immune system might well have built up antibodies to the sperm themselves. The antibodies will kill the sperm before they are fully mature. The tubes are open, but the manufacturing plant is dead. This cannot be fixed. Sadly, male sterility is permanent most of the time and can cause the loss of our hopes and dreams.

Because sperm are so numerous, if you are shipping or freezing, it is completely appropriate to do two collections, approximately an hour apart. The second collection will not have quite as much sperm in it, but it will have roughly 70-80% of what the first collection had and 70% of 400 million is quite a significant number. Try to do your shipped collections in this way, particularly if you are only going to be able to do one shipment. If your shipments are spaced over two days, you can easily do a collection, followed by a second collection after an hour and you have almost doubled the number of sperm that you can ship. You can do this for both collections and increase the number of good quality sperm.

The life span of a sperm is variable and is dependent upon what is done to it between ejaculation and death. Frozen sperm, once thawed and placed into the bitch have a life span of approximately 1-2 hours. Fresh chilled sperm will have a life span of about 12 hours after placement in the bitch. Fresh sperm, whether inseminated or placed by natural breeding will live at least 4-6 days. Some studies have found living sperm in the reproduction tract of a bitch 10 days or so following a breeding. Of course there is no way of assessing its quality, but it was alive.

Sperm are very fragile organisms. First, they must leave their place of origin and travel in unknown and hostile territory to search for the eggs. They are, of necessity, easily distracted and attracted to any round, smooth object that they find on the way to the eggs. There is a lot of competition when you are one of some 300 million to one billion sperm. Treat your stud dogs like gold. Feed them a great diet. Protect them from bad weather. Provide them with good dental care to prevent infections, abscesses and gum diseases that could lead to systemic disease and sterility. View their sperm as an invaluable resource and guard it once you have it in your care. Your next Best in Show winner depends on it.

Notes:

4- Artificial Insemination... "AI"

More Than One Way to Skin a Cat

If your dog or bitch is:

Already Injured; or

Aggressively Inclined; or

Amorously Indifferent; or

Anatomically Imperfect; or

Anxiously Intimidated; or

Aromatically Inexperienced; or just plain

Ain't Interested...

and if you intend to use that particular animal in your breeding program, you will probably need to utilize the techniques of Artificial Insemination. There is, indeed, more than one way to skin a cat, and artificial insemination is just one more way that you can deliver the sperm of the dog to the egg of the bitch. Certainly, a case can be made for eliminating every dog or bitch that is not an eager little beaver when it comes to breeding, but not all breeders want to eliminate a dog or bitch from a breeding program simply because they are unable to accomplish a natural breeding.

This chapter will discuss some of the reasons why a breeder may choose artificial insemination over a natural breeding. You are going to learn how to collect semen from the dog and how to inseminate a bitch. You will know how to find and use the equipment and tools necessary to complete an artificial insemination. Almost everything that you will need to collect and inseminate can be purchased from a grocery store, from the International Canine Sperm Bank, Camelot Farms, or in other online locations.

Already Injured

Dogs that are unable to complete a natural breeding due to injury may still be useful in your breeding program. The condition may be permanent or temporary but an injury is not a sign or symptom of a genetic imperfection no matter how long the effects from the injury last. If the dog has qualities that are valuable to the breed or to your particular breeding program then by all means, use the dog. By learning how to collect sperm and inseminate the bitch, you can safely use this dog for breeding. Already Injured dogs can be used in your breeding program with the use of AI.

Anatomically Imperfect

My most popular stud dog is a compact, well-built fifteen-pound boy. His services are often requested for those 20-pound bitches that may be rather long on the leg. He is very useful for sizing down and shaping up a bitch. However, once he began to service outside bitches, it quickly became obvious to me that I either had to build him a little ladder from which he could hang to breed these bitches or learn to do artificial inseminations. He took serious umbrage to having his tender little private parts handled by a stranger, so I had to learn to collect him myself. It was uncomfortable at first and a little bit scary, but many dogs will collect better and more willingly for their owner than for a vet. Many vets are not as practiced at collecting as the owner of a stud dog whose dance card is full. Being Anatomically Imperfect does not mean genetically malformed. Dogs and bitches are not always size compatible. Are you going to toss the structurally beautiful boy because he is a tad on the small side? Are you going to "pet out" the otherwise lovely girl because she is a little on the large side? Not if you are smart—and not if you understand the concepts of breeding, genetics and the gene pool.

Some bitches may have strictures that prevent a natural breeding, but may or may not interfere with the whelping process. She may well produce your "Best in Show" puppy. As a breeder, you must look to the general overall quality of the dog and then make the decision as to what the dog can add to the quality of the puppies produced. If the dog or bitch is Anatomically Imperfect, it may only mean that you need to have the skills necessary to collect your dog and inseminate your bitch. They may still be used in your breeding program.

Amorously Indifferent, Aggressively Inclined, Aromatically Inexperienced, Anxiously Intimidated and just plain Ain't Interested:

There will be times when your dog or bitch will be Amorously Indifferent to the breeding chore to which you have assigned them. Bitches that have developed "crushes" on specific stud dogs may be resistant to the boy that you have chosen for her. When breeding time arrives, she may be quite resistant to the advances of the boy you have chosen as her paramour. She may be Amorously Indifferent to your preferred stud dog while wildly waving her bottom toward "Boyfriend #1". She may even be Aggressively Inclined toward the boy you have chosen, threatening to take his little face off if he attempts to mount her.

Similarly, I have owned boys who were very lukewarm on the breeding process when presented with elderly bitches or bitches who have had known repro problems in the past. If your stud dog tells you NO… chances are good that he may have a valid reason for doing so. He simply Ain't Interested, and

20

only he knows the reason why. Don't forget: Contrary to how humans function, dogs breed to reproduce, and not for recreational purposes. If he says NO... it probably has a lot less to do with libido and a lot more to say about his little nose. Stud dogs have an amazing nose. They are not born with it; it requires education and experience to develop. A good stud dog is not going to waste his time and energy mounting and trying to breed a bitch that does not have eggs ready for fertilization. He may not choose to waste a breeding on eggs that he fertilized a couple of days ago. He will sniff and lick the vulva of the bitch vigorously in an effort to gather information. He may mount her to check her readiness and her reaction. If you watch a good stud dog in action, his behaviors will tell you more than you can ever learn on your own. His nose will tell him if eggs are there. His nose will tell him if the eggs are mature enough to warrant a breeding, and his nose will tell him if the eggs have already died. Of course, you have to give him time to mature and get over his infatuation with his stuffed toys and not all stud dogs learn the meaning of "restraint".

Younger, less experienced stud dogs may be a little less reliable. He may be <u>A</u>nxiously <u>I</u>ntimidated by an older, more dominant bitch. The older stud dogs may have let him know several times that the bitches are "theirs" and that his advances to them are most definitely unwelcome. That too can create <u>A</u>nxious <u>I</u>ntimidation. He may not have developed the "nose" for breeding that experience will give him and he is, therefore, <u>A</u>romatically <u>I</u>nexperienced. All of these problems can be overcome by the use of <u>Artificial Insemination</u>.

The Collection Process
Make sure that the dog has recently urinated before the collection process begins. Techniques vary depending on the size of the dog. There is a considerable difference between collecting sperm from a 15-pound cavalier when compared to collecting sperm from a 150-pound mastiff. My job is to give you the general overall picture of collecting and your job is to discuss the process with other breeders who have dogs who are similar to the size of your dog and adjust the techniques as necessary. I wish that I could give you very clear instructions on collecting a Mastiff, for instance, but I have not yet had the opportunity to work with a dog that large. Other breeders can fill in the blanks that I may leave.

Small dogs and even some medium dogs can be collected on a counter top or a grooming table. There is actually a valid reason for doing this aside from the fact that it is a gentler, kinder position for the aging breeder. (That would be me.) If you place the dog on the surface on which you will be collecting him from the time he is a puppy, and if you gently stroke his prepuce until he begins to get erect and then praise him and give him a treat, he will learn to associate that specific location with the act of feeling good. It is only a couple of clicks past that point to get him where you can collect his sperm in that specific location and make it a good experience for him. Praise your boy when his behaviors approach those that you are seeking. Let him know that he is doing the right thing.

I have always used a counter top, covered with a little non-slip throw rug. When my boys see me putting the rug on the counter top in the dog room… they know it is time for a collection. They will sniff the bitch and get very excited, but for the most part, if they see the rug on the counter top, they will not attempt a natural breeding. They know from experience that this is "AI" time. For larger breeds, you can collect on the floor, or you can use a small stool. I have collected larger breeds for friends, and used a small stool or chair so that I had easy access to the penis of the dog. You can sit directly on the floor if you are comfortable doing that (and can get up off the floor when you have finished). Try to figure out a way to position yourself so that you have good visual access to the penis of the dog and you are somewhat comfortable. You will need a second person to assist you by holding the bitch. Your most successful collections will be those using a teaser bitch. Often the teaser bitch is the bitch that is going to be inseminated, but not always.

The Teaser Bitch
If the stud dog has already rejected the bitch that is to be inseminated, she most likely will not make a suitable teaser bitch. You should, nevertheless, try using her first since you know she is in season and should have the right "smell". If you have another girl who is in season, you can use her as a teaser bitch, and then inseminate the intended mother-to-be with the sperm that you have collected. If you don't have another girl in season, you still have other options. If you have a mother who has recently delivered pups and is nursing, she may do well as a teaser bitch if you are quick and don't let the boy have a lot of time with her before he catches on that she only smells different because she is nursing. The key to using a girl who is not in season is that the dog must not have had access to her nor have seen her for several days. If you have her in place on the counter and then bring him to her, he will often mount her after a quick sniff or two just "because"… don't ask me why, but he will. She is "new", she is in place at the collection site well known to the stud dog, and she smells different.

Another very helpful tool is to use cotton-tipped applicator and swab them lightly around inside the vulvas of the girls who are in full-blown season and then freeze them inside a little sandwich baggy. Collect and save swabs on every girl who comes in season in your little group, and you will soon have several of them frozen and ready for use during the collection process. Thaw them for a few minutes at room temperature and use them to swab around on the rear end of the teaser bitch. DO NOT INSERT THEM INTO THE VULVA OF THE BITCH. Simply swab them around the rear end of the girl you are using as a teaser bitch. If you use a "teaser swab" on a nursing mom who has been separated from the stud dogs for several days, you will have remarkable success. It is probably the variety of different smells that does it, but it often results in a successful collection. If, however, you give the stud dog much time to do a complete exam, he will soon figure out that this bitch is really just his old friend, Sally, who has recently given birth and is nursing her puppies. The element of surprise is on your side.

Allow the dog to do some sniffing. If he does not then mount the bitch, gently stroke his prepuce a few times until you feel him begin to get an erection. If size allows, you can lift him into the mounting position to encourage him. Usually, just allowing him a few sniffs and then stroking his prepuce will give him the idea. Most of the time, you don't have to do anything to get him to mount the bitch. Once he mounts the bitch, you will need to 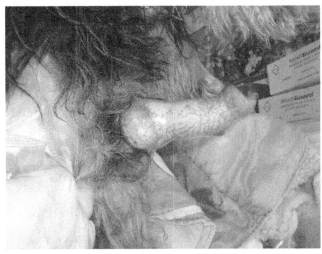 quickly place the collection bag over his penis and with one smooth movement, using the bag, push the prepuce up and behind the bulb. Reach your hand under the abdomen of the dog and quickly slide the collection bag up the penis, pushing the prepuce behind the bulb as you place the bag.

THE PREPUCE MUST BE BEHIND THE BULB, OR THE DOG CANNOT BECOME FULLY ERECT AND THE PROCESS CAN BE VERY, VERY PAINFUL FOR HIM. DO NOT ALLOW HIM TO BECOME ERECT INSIDE OF THE PREPUCE.

What you are doing during this process is letting your hand mimic the "feel" of the vagina. Hold his penis so that you can put slight pressure behind the bulb of the penis. Warm your hand first.

You are not massaging or stroking the penis. You are actually doing nothing but putting slight pressure behind the bulb and mimicking the feeling of the vagina by holding the penis and bulb. Do not confuse collection of a stud dog with masturbation. They are not the same. Once the dog begins the thrusting actions, you are pretty much assured of getting a collection. Continue holding the penis until you have collected the entire sperm fraction and some of the prostate fluid, no more than 5-6 ccs or so total.

The prostate fluid is clear, like water. The sperm fraction is very thick and milky white. When the two are mixed, the semen is cloudy but thinned out and watery. If you are not quite gentle with it, it will develop bubbles that are difficult to get out of your insemination rod. Learn to estimate what five ccs of fluid looks like in your collection bag. GENTLY remove the collection bag from the penis, and put the dog away in a safe, solitary environment. Check him after a few minutes to make sure that the penis has retracted safely into the prepuce. If it hasn't, gently pull on the hair around the prepuce and urge it to come over the end of the penis. It is possible to collect a stud dog without a teaser bitch but some studies have shown that there will be less sperm in the collection. If you want to maximize the quantity of the collection, use a teaser bitch if possible.

When collecting sperm from small and medium sized dogs, you can use Playtex® baby bottle inserts. Use the variety that is labeled: "Drop-Ins". These have a firm plastic top that holds the bag open for ease in placing the bag onto the penis. They are 5.5 inches long and 2 inches wide across the top. They have a capacity of 8 oz. If they are not large enough for your breed of dog, you will need to purchase collection sleeves from 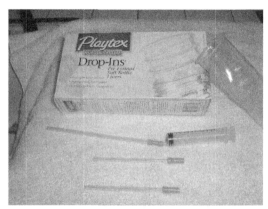 Camelot Farms, the International Canine Sperm Bank (ICSB) or other sources on the Internet.

The Insemination Process

Make sure that the bitch has been walked and has emptied her bladder prior to the insemination process. Some bitches can be inseminated with only one person present, but it is always best, and safest, to have a second person present to assist you in holding the bitch while you do the insemination. The best insemination tool is an insemination rod, which can be purchased from Camelot Farms, ICSB, or other sites on the internet. Some people use soft, flexible catheters, but these are not as useful (as discussed below), and often contain latex which is toxic to sperm. Use a rod of the correct length for your breed of dog. ICSB will fill your order based on the breed of dog that you list on the order form. The rods come in sizes from 4 inches long to about 14 inches long. If you can only obtain the longer ones, you can cut them to fit and use an open flame on the edges to smooth them over. It is easier to try to buy the correct size from the beginning. Oddly enough, these rods are the same diameter as the rods used to inseminate horses and cattle; only the lengths will differ for different breeds of dogs.

The rod must have a connector. Usually this is a small piece of flexible plastic tubing. This connector is vitally important because it connects the rod and the syringe. Rods and syringes do not fit together without the use of the connector. The fact that it is flexible is important and allows more manipulation of the rod as you try to find the perfect position for the placement of the sperm. You will need syringes of approximately 6-20 ccs capacity, labeled "latex free". You should use a new rod and syringe for

24

each bitch. Do not re-use your equipment on other bitches. After you have completed all of the AIs for that particular bitch, throw the rod and the syringe away. Clean it between AIs by rinsing well in very hot water, following that rinse by a rinse in normal saline solution and then allowing to completely air dry before using it for a second or third breeding. A sunny windowsill is a great place for air-drying.

Following the collection:

Attach the syringe to the connector on the insemination rod. Pull the semen into the syringe by putting the end of the rod directly into the semen in the collection bag. Holding the syringe and rod pointing upward and against the light, gently push out all of the air from the syringe and rod, pushing the semen almost to the end of the rod. Do not expel semen from the rod… remember, each drop has thousands and thousands of sperm in it… one may be the best pup you've ever produced!

Drop a single drop of semen on a slide, cover it with a cover slip and using the instructions for your microscope, look at the semen. You want to make sure they are alive and very active. Practice with the microscope well in advance of the collection/insemination process. Be familiar with this valuable

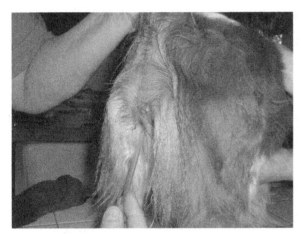

piece of equipment. You can often find them on eBay for a very reasonable price (see http://www.ebay.com). Binocular microscopes are easier to use than monocular ones.

After you have taken a quick look at the semen, you are ready for the insemination. At this point, you should have a syringe and a rod with semen in both the syringe and the rod and no air except for very small bubbles in the syringe or insemination rod. With someone holding the front end of the bitch,

(muzzled if necessary for safety) insert the rod into the vulva of the bitch. Insert the rod going UP into the vulva, aiming toward the spine. The rod should be almost parallel to the legs. Do not attempt to insert the rod going straight into the vulva. The vulva and vagina are shaped rather like an upside down L. Insert the rod upwards into the vulva until you feel it come to the dead end, which would be up next to the spine. Then, using the firmness of the

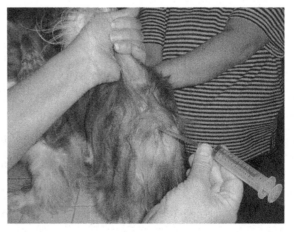

rod, simply LIFT the rod upwards until the rod is now pointed straight into the vulva and gently move the rod forward. This "lifting" action is why a flexible insemination rod is not desirable. You need the firmness of the rod to "lift" the vulva so that the rod can then go straight in toward the cervix. Advance the rod gently into the vagina until you cannot advance it further. Once you have done this a few times, you will begin to learn the correct depth for the size of bitch that you are inseminating.

If the placement of the rod falls short of the depth that is appropriate for your bitch, try a few things to see if you can advance it further. Hold her up, with her front paws on the counter or floor and her back legs up in the air. Try again to advance the rod. If this doesn't work, gently rotate one of her back legs out away from the body while her back legs are in the air. If this doesn't work, let her stand on all four legs again and, taking turns with each leg, gently rotate out each of her rear legs from her body and try to advance the rod again. Once you have inserted the rod as far as it will go, hold the bitch with her back feet in the air and, using the plunger of the syringe, place all of the semen into the bitch. (Of course, you may not be able to lift the back legs of a very large dog and might want to construct a slanted table for use during inseminations. After the semen has been placed within the body of the bitch. quickly disconnect the syringe from the connector, pull one cc of air or normal saline into the syringe, reconnect the syringe on to the connector and push the one cc of air or saline into the body of the bitch. This is done to clear all of the semen out of the rod. Every single drop of semen contains thousands of sperm and you want every one of them to have an equal opportunity to fertilize the eggs.

After you have placed the semen into the body of the bitch, quickly withdraw the rod and place your finger into the vulva. Lightly massage this area and you will often feel a "clasping" sort of action. This action is an indication that the bitch's body is 'pulling' the semen up into her uterus. If, as you stroke the vulva, you also see it lift slightly or "wink", you also can rest assured that the timing for this breeding is good. Continue to hold the bitch with her feet in the air and massage the vulva for five minutes. Place the bitch in a Vari Kennel® and leave her there for a couple of hours. Re-inseminate her again the next day or on the second day after. Time the AIs just as you would a natural breeding.

Myths about AI:
Myth number one: Artificial Inseminations result in smaller litters.
Some breeders feel that Artificial Inseminations result in smaller litters. I doubt this. I've known breeders who had a single puppy with several natural ties and I've known breeders (me for one) who have had nine pups with a single AI. If the sperm is healthy, the timing is right, and the placement of the semen is good, there in no reason why an AI can't result in a normal sized litter. Again, we are back to the question of which of the dogs involved in the breeding is responsible for the size of the litter. The bitch has dutifully produced 1-12 eggs once or twice a year and the dog has dutifully

26

produced at least 300-400 million sperm for EVERY ejaculate. Who do you think is responsible for the size of the litter? Do the math correctly here and you will come with the answer: the bitch.

Myth number two: Artificial Inseminations result in more "missed" breedings.

I think that this is correct. However, I don't believe it is because the breeding was done by artificial insemination. It is correct because of whatever was happening that created the situation that required the AI. If the stud dog refused the bitch, he may have known there were no eggs present. If the bitch refused the breeding, she may have known that the timing was way off. They can't talk to us in words, but their actions can teach us many, many things if we learn to listen. If we were required to accomplish a breeding by means of Artificial Insemination, it is usually because we were unable to get a natural breeding. The Artificial Insemination itself did not cause the missed breeding. The reason *behind* the artificial insemination caused the missed breeding. Things get even trickier when you start thinking about using chilled or frozen sperm.

Fresh Chilled and Extended Sperm

Luckily for dog breeders, sperm has a very long life span when compared to that of other mammals. They may well be delicate, but they live quite a long while. (Yes, I know... delicate, but long-lived, sort of an oxymoron, but what do you do? It is true.) Dog breeders commonly use sperm shipped in from other states. The method used to bring sperm from a dog in Studville, East Coast to a bitch in Bitchcity, West Coast is to first collect the fresh sperm, spin it carefully in a centrifuge, remove the prostatic fluid, replace a portion of it with extender and chill for shipping. Commercially manufactured extenders are available for us as well as homemade ones. Homemade extenders may contain skim milk, cream, egg yolk, and liquid antibiotics. Egg yolk is used in almost all homemade extenders as a buffer to protect the sperm. Chilling the sperm decreases both its motility and lifespan. This single fact is the most important thing to understand when using chilled sperm. *Some of the sperm will either die or be made inactive by the chilling and none of them will live as long as when they were fresh.* By all means, try to obtain a second collection an hour after the first collection when you intend to ship. Most stud dogs will be fine with it, and you will have increased the number of sperm shipped by about 70%. It will not hurt the dog, nor his fertility, but it will increase the numbers of sperm for the stud fee.

The ideal situation is over-night shipping and insemination the day following collection. Studies have shown that fresh chilled sperm can be inseminated at 48 hours of age, but with definite loss of quality. Timing for an insemination using fresh chilled, extended sperm is critical. The sperm has a dependable life span after insemination of approximately 12 hours. It is necessary to do frequent progesterone tests on the bitch to determine the day of ovulation. Because the eggs take two full days to ripen, you should not introduce fresh chilled sperm into the bitch until you know that the eggs are ripe and ready for fertilization. This is how you can plan for the insemination of fresh chilled sperm:

The bitch ovulates a primary oocyte (egg) when her progesterone level reaches approximately five ng/ml. The primary oocyte has a lifespan of approximately two to three days. It matures into a secondary oocyte which lives somewhere in the neighborhood of 24-36 hours. Fresh sperm, either from a natural breeding or a direct dog to bitch insemination has a life span of at least 5 days, probably longer. Therefore, if a dog breeds a bitch naturally even two or three days before she ovulates, clearly the sperm will still be viable and fully able to fertilize the egg after it has gone through the primary stages and is a fully mature secondary oocyte. Fresh chilled and extended sperm has a much shorter life span particularly after it has been inseminated into the bitch, as the chilling decreases its life span. Don't count on fresh chilled sperm to live longer than 12 hours once it has been collected, chilled, shipped, warmed and inseminated. Time your insemination for somewhere around 55-65 hours after the progesterone level reached five ng/ml. Discuss with your vet the most advantageous method to place the sperm closest to the ripened eggs. Your vet may recommend a routine artificial insemination, a transcervical insemination (requires special equipment and skill to thread the rod through the cervix and into the uterus), or surgical implantation (uterine horn is directly inseminated after being lifted from the abdomen). Here are the basics to remember when planning an insemination with chilled sperm:

- The sperm must be in good quality to begin with, and it will lose quality due to chilling.
- The timing of ovulation and the maturity of the eggs is critical.
- The route chosen for insemination must take into account the life span of the chilled sperm. They can only go so far and get there so fast before they start dying off.

Insemination with Frozen Sperm

The use of frozen canine sperm has been equally fraught with difficulties. Dairy cattle were routinely being inseminated with frozen sperm by the late 1950's. The success rate was good, and dairy farmers were delighted that they now had an alternative to keeping a dangerously bad-tempered bull on the farm. In addition to being able to get rid of their bull, which frequently tore down fences and terrorized the neighbors, they were now able to choose from a catalogue of the best producing bulls in the US. (Incidentally, "best producing" bulls are bulls whose daughters produce the most milk per month.) Wouldn't you know that a male would even get the credit for the best milk production?

It wasn't until 1981 that the AKC registered its first puppy sired by frozen sperm. Many of the early failures with frozen canine sperm were due to the much-shortened life span of the thawed sperm. Originally, the frozen sperm (once thawed) was vaginally inseminated. Of course, since the life span of frozen sperm is approximately one to two hours… the failure rate was huge. We are back to the original premise: the sperm can only go so far and get there so fast before they start dying off, and when they have been frozen, they die even faster than when they were chilled. In order to maximize your chances of getting a successful litter from frozen sperm, you will need to have a skilled vet perform a surgical insemination. The uterine horns are lifted from the abdomen and palpated to check for cysts and other abnormalities. Surgical implantations are done only a single time; not repeated each day as vaginal inseminations can be. The vet will often be able to break down cysts during the palpation of the horns and following the procedure, they will have a good idea of the condition of the uterine horns. When using frozen sperm, the timing for insemination is even more critical than when using fresh chilled. According to Dr. Cindy Smith, our well-known and much-revered canine reproduction specialist practicing in Washington State, the timing for the surgical implantation of frozen sperm is at its optimum at 68-72 hours following ovulation. Using her technique and timing guidelines she has a much higher than usual rate of success using frozen sperm.

By now, you have undoubtedly noticed the frequent use of words and terms like probably, approximately, most likely, around, in the neighborhood, etc. The reason for this vague terminology is that the canine reproductive system is rather complex and unpredictable when compared to other mammals. As proof of this, look at the success of cloning dogs versus cloning other mammals. Sheep, cattle, horses, cats, mice and human tissue were all cloned before a dog was successfully cloned. The first mammal cloned was a sheep born in 1997. Years of research followed before finally in 2005, two puppies were cloned after 1000 cloned canine eggs were implanted into several bitches. (One puppy died shortly after birth.) Scientists who ultimately succeeded in cloning a dog attributed their many failures to the nature of the canine egg. The eggs were elusive and the life span was poorly understood and poorly manipulated. One of the reasons that the reproductive system of the dog presents so many challenges is that bitches come into season once or twice per year. Cattle, horses, sheep, and humans produce eggs (or "come into season") about every 28 days. Dogs produce eggs once or twice per year. Unlike other mammals, the bitch also produces primary oocytes that require two to three days of ripening before they can be fertilized. Most mammals ovulate eggs which are ready for fertilization at the time of their release. All of these differences have combined to create a rather complex and delicate reproductive system in the canine. This fact is hard to believe when the one breeding that you didn't plan is the only one that results in pups, but true nonetheless.

5- Vaginal Swabs and Cultures
The Hunt for Tiny Livestock

All of us carry tiny livestock. We all harbor bacteria, sometimes even viruses and yeast. They are everywhere. They are on our skin, in our mouths, in hair follicles; you name it…microbes are probably either living in it, have lived in it or will set up housekeeping in it in the future. The key factor isn't whether or not they are present; it is whether or not they are causing disease. Not all microorganisms are "pathogenic" (cause diseases). Some are simply part of the resident flora and fauna of a living system. In other words, they live there but they tend to their business and don't cause problems.

In our society, there is a lot of talk about sexually transmitted diseases. It used to be that the phrase was used only in relationship to human sexually transmitted diseases. Now we know that there are sexually transmitted diseases present in the canine community as well, but not as many as you may have been led to believe. Much more common than sexually transmitted diseases are microorganisms that are present in the reproductive tract of the bitch which are responsible for many reproductive problems. These organisms, although they reside in the reproductive tract of the bitch, are not considered sexually transmitted. Sexually transmitted would mean that it is a disease process (not simply a trading of bacteria) that is passed from one of the breeding partners to the other during the act of natural breeding. Unless your girl has had reproduction problems in the past, you don't necessarily need to worry about these organisms. Reproductive problems would be an indication for a trip to a vet to request a swab and culture of cranial vagina. These are some, but not necessarily all of the reproductive problems that you might have encountered:

- Missed breedings when the bitch appeared receptive but missed
- Miscarriages or abortions (used interchangeably)
- Absorption
- Fetal Demise in utero
- Puppies dead on arrival or shortly thereafter
- True prematurely (based on progesterone levels, not days of breedings)

If you have experienced these things with one or more of your girls, they may be harboring a microorganism that can be controlled with a medication given by your vet. This chapter is about the culture swabs and the microbes that may very well be on them. The terms that you need to understand in order to understand all of the information contained here are as follows:

- **Cranial Vagina**: The end of the vagina that is closest to the bitch's head
- **Caudal Vagina**: The end of the vagina that is closest to the bitch's tail
- **Prepuce**: The sheath of fur covered skin that covers the penis
- **Aerobic bacteria**: Bacteria that grow in the presence of oxygen
- **Anaerobic bacteria**: Bacteria that will not grow in the presence oxygen
- **Virus**: Another one of the guilty parties that can cause diseases. They aren't discovered on a vaginal swab since the technique for growing them differs significantly from the techniques used to grow bacteria
- **Yeast**: Another one of the microorganisms that can cause problems. They like warm, dark, moist places and proliferate in an atmosphere that is high in glucose (which is why diabetics are so susceptible to yeast infections)
- **Culture:** The swab will collect material that will be placed on a culture dish to "grow out" cultures of the microorganisms for identification and also to see what will kill them
- **"Hooded" or "guarded" culture swabs**: In order for the vet to correctly swab the cranial vagina, it is necessary to use a "hooded" or "guarded" swab. The end of the swab is covered and once in the correct position can be uncovered to collect the culture. This will avoid contaminating the culture by the many different types of bacteria that are living near the caudal end of the vagina
- **Fetus or Fetal**: A puppy still in the uterus
- **Neonatal**: A newborn puppy
- **Abortion or Miscarriage**: These are used interchangeably
- **Mummification, or Mummy Puppies**: Pups that die during the development period but are not aborted. They are usually smaller than newborns, brownish in color, and firm. They look like puppies with intact body parts but have been dead for some period of time

Now that you have the terminology, we can begin our discussion. This may come as a surprise to you, but the only sexually transmitted bacteria that is known for a certainty to cause sterility/infertility in the canine population is ***Brucella Canis***. That's right. It is Brucella, and you won't find it using a routine vaginal swab; only by having blood drawn for the serology test that is specific for Brucella. Herpes can be venerally transmitted, but it won't cause sterility or infertility, only neonatal disease and/or death. Mycoplasma may cause reproduction problems and fetal death, but it won't cause sterility.

Only Brucella is known to infect an otherwise healthy, virile, fertile dog and render it sterile. Bitches should be tested for Brucella yearly and frequently used stud dogs every six months. Brucella is associated to a certain degree with cattle, so dogs that are around farms may need to be tested more frequently. So what about all of the other bacteria and viruses that we all hear about? What are they, where are they, and what are they doing?

The most common bacteria found are Pasteurella multocida, Beta-hemolytic streptococci and E-coli. Even though these are the most common, Staph and Bacillus are relatively common as well. The numbers of bacteria that can be isolated are at their most numerous during proestrous and estrous. Some of these are common enough and create enough repro problems that I want to discuss them with you, but studies on others have been inconclusive or they are so rare that they do not warrant space here. I want to talk to you about common problems—not rare ones.

Discuss with your vet the appropriate timing for the culture. The vet may recommend waiting until she is in season when they are most numerous, or may recommend doing a vaginal swab at a time between seasons. If the bitch has had reproductive problems in the past and the culture reveals that she is harboring bacteria that have a history of causing reproductive problems, follow the treatment recommended by your vet. Unless you have experienced reproductive problems, it is not wise to try to kill off the microorganisms living within her reproductive tract.

As the antibiotics kill off these organisms, which have not shown themselves to be a problem, they will also kill off the flora and fauna that are normal for her particular reproduction tract. This will upset the normal balance within her reproductive tract and could well leave her more vulnerable to infection from other sources. This same thing happens with human patients. Women who are on antibiotics will frequently develop vaginal yeast infections. Why? Because the antibiotics have killed off the bacteria in their vaginas and the yeast are then left unchallenged to grow and flourish. Voila! Yeast Infection Heaven! The antibiotic has disturbed the normal day-to-day balance of the flora and fauna of the vagina and yeast are then able to proliferate. What are some of the normal, day-to-day organisms that are living within the reproductive tract of the bitch?

Studies have shown that roughly 60 percent of all normal, healthy bitches have _aerobic_ bacteria in the cranial vagina and about 90 percent of all normal, healthy bitches have _aerobic_ bacteria in the caudal vagina. It makes sense that there would be more bacteria in the caudal vagina since that is the area nearest the rear end of the bitch; the area that the bitch sits on... sits on at dog shows, sits on in the dirt in your backyard and sidewalks in your neighborhood as you chat with your neighbor when you walk

32

your girl in the morning. Doesn't really take much imagination to guess how those bacteria got there. It's only a hop, skip and a jump to the cranial vagina, so it doesn't take a rocket scientist to figure out how those microorganisms got further up into the cranial vagina either.

Anaerobic bacteria are also found in the vaginas of normal, healthy bitches. These bacteria can often be seen on vaginal smears, but not found on culture dishes because of their anaerobic nature (they won't grow in the presence of oxygen). The anaerobic bacteria that the bitch may house can include Peptococcaeceae, Lactobacillus, Bifidobacterium, Clostridium, Corynebacterium, and Haemophilus. Mycoplasma can also live within the bitch's vagina. Mycoplasma was found in almost 75% of the bitches in one study. In another study, 90% of the bitches who were swabbed were found to be housing Mycoplasma.

The microorganisms that are living in the reproductive tract of the bitch are not sexist in nature. They aren't particular about the gender of where they hang their hats. Just about any place is home to bacteria. When a dog's prepuces are cultured, guess what? They harbor just about the same kinds of bacteria in just about the same numbers that the bitches are housing. Because the stud dogs aren't the ones miscarrying litters or delivering dead puppies, we tend to forget all about them when we discuss swabs and cultures—when we are on our hunt for tiny livestock. They also, however, carry around many of the little freeloaders. Moreover, if you have a culture swab done on the prepuce of the stud dog that has pulled up sterile, are the microorganisms you find guilty of having made him sterile? NO. The only microorganism known beyond a shadow of a doubt to cause sterility is brucella, and you won't find it on a culture swab.

So to answer the original questions… What are they? Where are they? And, what are they doing? The answer appears to be something like this:

- They are bacteria, both aerobic and anaerobic.
- They are viruses.
- Less frequently, they are yeast.
- They are everywhere and they appear to serve no actual purpose other than to be part of the normal every day flora and fauna of the reproductive tract of the bitch and the dog.
- They may actually serve a function but that function is unknown to us.
- Their only function may be to act as a check and balance system on each other.

- We don't really know what they are doing there unless they cause problems, but under some circumstances, they certainly cause disease and reproduction problems.
- The only <u>sexually transmitted</u> bacterium that is definitely associated with canine sterility is brucella. Other diseases may be sexually transmitted…but they won't cause sterility.
- Even when culture swabs were collected from bitches with known reproductive diseases, the results were very similar to the results of swabs collected from normal, healthy bitches.

Herpes:

Canine Herpesvirus Infection, or CHV, was first identified in 1965 as a cause of canine neonatal death. It isn't found on routine pre-breeding cultures because viral isolation is not a usual part of those routine tests. Tests specifically for viruses need to be utilized to isolate Herpes. Canine Herpes is spread in the air by infected dogs who are coughing, by direct contact with mouth, nasal and genital secretions and by breeding dogs that are infected. It is what I call a "Sniffy-Licky" disease. Being around affected animals who are coughing, sneezing, sniffing and licking appear to be more common causes than sexual transmission. In adult dogs, the disease is apparently very mild; sometimes not even detected, and it does not seem to affect fertility. It will kill your puppies in what seems like the blink of an eye.

The adult dog that is affected by herpes will have mild symptoms that are restricted to the respiratory tract, and/or the genital tract. Herpes, however, is devastating to puppies. Young bitches, and those who don't get out very often are most likely to develop it when exposed to an unusual environment. Older bitches that have been exposed to many other dogs at dog shows, dog parks and on frequent walks may have already been infected with herpes without your knowledge. Once you have decided to breed your bitch, stop showing her, stop walking her in the neighborhood and stop taking her to the dog park. A bitch that has recently been bred should not be taken into locations where she might be exposed to herpes. If you suspect that your bitch may have had herpes at some point, have your vet draw her blood and do a titer test on her. If she has already had herpes…you have one less thing to worry about. Leave pregnant bitches home for the duration of the gestation except for trips to the vet.

If a pregnant bitch develops herpes while she is pregnant, you can take it to the bank that you will lose most, if not all of that litter. The virus will spread to the fetus and it will wreak havoc. Herpes in the unborn puppies can cause fetal death, abortion, prematurity, and mummies. If the puppies are born alive, they will die in large numbers. At least two-thirds of all puppies born to recently infected bitches will die. Until a newborn puppy has reached the age of 3 weeks, it is unable to mount a fever response to the virus. Studies have shown that the virus can be killed by a temperature three degrees above normal over a 2-3 day period. The virus can also be killed by antibodies to the virus that were developed by dogs that had the disease at some point in their lives. No treatment has been shown to be truly useful, possibly because the puppies die within 24-48 hours after showing the first signs of infection. By the time the puppy appears to be sick, it is too late for treatment.

A puppy who has herpes will not nurse well. It may cry, have diarrhea, and a runny nose. If I had a litter that had those signs and symptoms, and if I wished to be as aggressive as possible in saving my puppies, I would do several things:

- Increase the body temperature of the puppies to 100 degrees.
- Take rectal temperatures to make sure that the puppies bodies are at that temperature.
- Utilize the techniques of tube feeding and/or sub-cutaneous hydration to keep them hydrated.
- Increase the humidity in their environment a little bit to offset the drying nature of the extra heat.
- Administer oxygen to my puppies to avoid as much cellular death and damage as possible.
- Take some of my older dogs, the ones who have been to dog shows and dog parks… those who might have had the disease and developed antibodies to it, to see the vet. I would ask my vet to draw blood from two or three of my older, most "experienced" dogs, spin it down to a clear serum, and inject the clear serum into my puppies. If they had herpes in the past…all the better.

If the vet could hit a vein and inject it intravenously, perfect. Injecting it sub cutaneously is better than nothing. Your chances of saving your pups are probably pretty slim, but if you wish to be aggressive and try to save your puppies, the things listed above <u>might</u> work. The herpes antibodies work something like this: They put out the signal to the immune system that help is needed. The immune system sends white blood cells to the infected sites and the white blood cells 'engulf' the virus.

The good news about herpes infection is that once your bitch has had the disease, she is usually done with it. Canine herpes is not like human genital herpes. It does not recur repeatedly. Once they have it, they are finished with it, they have developed antibodies and it does not affect future breedings. It may kill a litter that she is carrying at the time that she develops the disease, but it will not affect her fertility and does not appear to affect future litters. My book, <u>Puppy Intensive Care</u>, will teach you how to tube feed, hydrate by sub cutaneous methods, and administer oxygen. Learning these techniques is easier than you might think and acquiring the necessary tools does not require a prescription from the vet. You will be grateful for the knowledge. If you are a breeder, you need these skills.

Beta Strep:

Beta-hemolytic streptococci, or Beta Strep for short, has been around forever. Pregnant humans have being swabbed for Beta Strep for at least 20 years, probably longer. We know that if a woman is harboring Beta Strep, she will not have symptoms of disease. We know that beta strep can cause infant mortality in the human population. We know that once a woman has it, she will have it for the length of her reproductive life. We know for a certainty that she will require treatment each time she is pregnant. If the mother is treated at time of delivery or shortly before, it will not create a problem for the newborn, but if left untreated, it can kill the new baby. This is the same as with dogs, except that we are only just now hearing about it. It is a common microorganism and it does not always cause problems. When it does cause problems, the problems it causes are huge.

Sometimes Beta Strep will affect only one bitch in a kennel. Other times, several bitches will be affected by it. It isn't exactly considered contagious... only one of my nine bitches harbored Beta Strep... but then again, it sometimes affects every bitch in a kennel. Certainly, the mode of transmission is unknown since almost all dogs harbor it. If a single bitch within your group of dogs, or if several bitches have had problems with general infertility, missed breedings, miscarriage (also called abortion) fetal demise in utero, or neonatal death, you need to ask your vet to do a hooded culture at the cranial vagina to look for Beta Strep on each affected bitch. Discuss with your vet the option of culturing one and, if positive, treating them all. At this time, hooded culture swabs are only manufactured for use in horses, so don't be overly alarmed when your vet walks into the exam room with a very, very long culture swab. It is probably a good idea for the vet to do what is called a "culture and sensitivity" lab test because not only will the organism be identified, but a list of the antibiotics that will treat it will be identified as well. Some of the antibiotics used for Beta Strep are Amoxicillin, Keflex and Baytril. Each bitch who has been identified as a carrier of Beta Strep and who has a history of reproduction problems will need to be treated at the first sign of her season for at least seven days and again at the end of her gestation for at least seven days. This will need to be done at the time of each breeding for her entire reproductive life. She may never show symptoms of having a disease process, but for some reason, the microorganism that she is carrying will cause problems with reproductive and fertility unless you treat her each time she is bred.

E-coli:

Escherichia coli is found in feces. Different strains of these bacteria are found in the feces of different species of animal, but it is all E-coli. It is the most common of all the microbes found when the bitch is cultured. Not surprisingly, it is also the perpetrator of most crimes within the bladder as well. It has been implicated in reproductive problems of the same type as Beta Strep, but less commonly.

36

Neomycin is a common antibiotic used to treat infections of E-coli, but your vet may have other treatment modalities. Again: only treat for E-coli if you have a history of reproductive difficulties within your kennel and your vet has determined that your problem is E-coli. Fecal materials shouldn't get caught in the fur of the rear end of our dogs, but it does. It shouldn't be able to work its way into the urethras, vulvas and prepuces of our dogs, but it does. Our dogs shouldn't eat feces, but they do. It's a wonder any of them survive doghood with its many encounters with E-coli, but they do.

Breeders need to use other ways to examine their breeding animals as well as using cultures and swabs. You may never have had repro problems, but you still want to be aware of potential problems and use good breeding practices and techniques to avoid problems within your kennel. Use your eyes and your nose to check each bitch that comes to your dog for breeding. Watch her as she eats, plays and interacts with other bitches. Does she eat normally? Does she play and behave as normal, healthy dogs behave? Check the color of her vaginal discharge by pressing a clean white tissue to her vulva. Smell the tissue. If you suspect that it smells "infected", get your nose up closer and actually sniff for odor. Infection will smell like meat that has gone bad. Once you smell it, you will never forget it. Take a rectal temperature. (The normal temperature should be in the neighborhood of 101.5 to 102.5 degrees Fahrenheit). Using your gloved hand, pull the tissues of the vulva apart and check for lesions. Gently run a gloved finger around the inside of the vulva. Do you feel bumps, or lesions? They shouldn't be there. If they are, it is time for a visit to your vet for diagnosis and treatment if available.

If you own a stud dog, check him using the same techniques from time to time. Pull back the prepuce and look at his penis. It should be a deep rose color, moist in appearance. It is quite vascular looking. It should not have blisters or open sores. Use a tissue to press against the end of the prepuce. Other than the musky, strong odor that all intact dogs have, there should be no unusual odor. The dog should not be spending an inordinate amount of time every day licking his penis. It is normal for him to lick his penis following a breeding, but not on a day to day basis. Is he eating normally? Does he lift his leg and mark around the yard without hesitation? Does he yelp when he urinates?) This not a good sign, incidentally; always bad) Take his temperature. Use all of your senses, including your common sense to examine the dog and the bitch. Remember, there is a difference between the presence of bacteria and the presence of disease. Disease must be present in order for disease to be spread.

To summarize the last several paragraphs: bacteria are always present in the reproduction tract of both the bitch and the dog. If you have a vaginal culture done, you will learn that bacteria of different types are present:

- You will not, however, find Brucella—the only known cause of canine sterility.

- You will not find Herpes, a known viral cause of puppy mortality, nor will you find other virus.
- You will not be able to detect anaerobic bacteria on a routine culture.

The bacteria that you will find are probably not causing a disease process unless your dog is showing signs and symptoms of disease and/or reproductive difficulties. Using an antibiotic to treat the normal bacteria that will be found in a normal, healthy bitch serves no purpose other than to disturb the day-to-day microbes that inhabit the reproduction tract of the animal. This can actually put your dog at risk in two ways: First, you will reduce the number of normal bacteria thus allowing abnormal populations to increase, and secondly, you will be putting your dog at risk for developing a sensitivity to the antibiotic, or worse, becoming immune to its benefits. Admittedly, becoming immune to antibiotics is not as much of a problem with dogs as human, but still something to consider. Humans have a much longer life span and so will have many more opportunities to develop immunities to different antibiotics. Treat your repro problems, but don't just arbitrarily treat the normal bacteria that are there.

Reproductive problems are obvious to you. You will have missed breedings, spontaneous abortions (miscarriages), dead puppies in utero or dead puppies in the whelping box, and prematurity. These problems will be unmistakable. If you see dark, greenish discharge well before time for the litter to be born, you may be looking at a dead puppy in utero. This is common in the canine, but can, nevertheless, cause the loss of an entire litter. Take your bitch to the vet at the first sign of foul discharge and if you both suspect that there is a dead puppy, ask them to put the bitch on a drug called Terbutaline and also ask for Baytril®. Terbutaline is a drug designed to relax smooth muscle of the uterus and lungs. It can prevent contractions in case the bitch is trying to abort the entire litter because of one or two dead pups. Baytril® is especially useful against bacteria such as the kind a dead puppy in utero would be growing. The combination of Terbutaline and Baytril can close the cervix, stop premature contractions and keep the risk of infection down to almost nothing. In a few days, your bitch will deliver her litter, but the dead puppy will not have caused her to abort the entire litter.

Abnormal behaviors, lethargy, loss of appetite, increased temperature, foul smelling discharge, excessive licking, coughing and other signs and symptoms of disease are right there before you. Use your common sense, your eyes, your nose and your sense of touch to give you the information that you need. If you have good reason to suspect that your dog or bitch may have a disease, have a swab done and follow the advice of your vet as to a treatment modality. Try to avoid the use of antibiotics unless they are truly indicated. Save them for those times when your dog needs antibiotics to save his or her life, not for routine prophylactic purposes. Here are things you can do to prevent some problems:

- If you own a stud dog, you should get into the habit of performing a little ritual after each breeding that can help to get rid of many of the transferred bacteria.

- Immediately after a tie, push back the prepuce of the dog and rinse his penis off using warm normal saline. A water bottle with the "sports bottle" top works very well for this.

- You can purchase sterile normal saline from pharmacies in 1000 cc bottles or you can make your own using my recipe: to 16 ounces of distilled water, add one teaspoon of plain, non-iodized salt and ½ teaspoon of baking soda. If you make your own, mix it often, preferably fresh for each use.

- After the dog has completed his breeding duties for any specific girl, add 5ccs of Betadyne® to that mixture. Depending on your preference, you can also use this mixture as a "douche" on the stud dog. Remember that almost anything will kill sperm and Betadyne® will probably kill it quicker than anything, so wait until his breeding duties for this specific girl are completed before you use the weak Betadyne® solution as a "douche".

- <u>Never use a douche on a bitch unless you are specifically instructed to do so by your vet</u>. You can "flush" bacteria into the uterus.

- While the dog is lying down, place the tip of the sports bottle at the opening of the prepuce and rinse the penis and surrounding tissues while they are inside the prepuce. The solution will not sting and if the temperature is about 95 degrees, the dog will not complain.

- Do not use plain water for this. Use your saline solution.

Do not use the Betadyne® solution prior to a breeding, and do not use it if the dog will be doing another breeding within two days. The Betadyne®/saline solution is fairly weak and mild, but used as a rinse, it can keep your dog clean without harming delicate tissue. Betadyne® will kill more microorganisms than anything else available, and unless there is an allergy to iodine, it is extremely safe. It is widely used in human surgery and can even be used full strength on wounds, although a weaker solution is more advisable. Full strength Betadyne® will kill just about variety of tiny livestock known to man, but will inhibit the growth of new cells in a wound even using a 10% solution.

Your own five senses, combined with the medical technology that your vet can offer gives you the best of both worlds. By utilizing everything that is at your fingertips, you will become a better breeder. You will be more successful in your hunt for tiny livestock and more successful at combating them. If you are in doubt about the safety of a specific natural breeding, learn how to collect sperm and inseminate artificially. Conveniently, I have written an entire chapter devoted specifically to that topic.

6- Progesterone

The Engine That Pulls the Reproduction Train

As the bitch approaches the time when she is coming into season, her progesterone level slowly begins to rise. Once she has shown her first sign of a season, usually bright red blood, other changes have started happening in her body as well. In order to prepare her for a natural breeding, with the entrance and thrusting of a male penis into her vagina, the delicate mucous membranes in her vagina have started the process of cornification. This means that a different type of skin cell is growing and layering inside the vagina. These skin cells are designed to protect her vaginal tissues from the penis at the time of breeding. These changes occur with each season for every bitch.

Females come into season anywhere from about six months of age until 24 months of age. Once a girl has come into season, that is the beginning of puberty. In the same way that humans are not ready yet for parenthood at the onset of puberty, neither are dogs. The age of onset for puberty varies greatly and does not seem to be related to size. The Bull Mastiff, which will weigh around 100-120 pounds when fully grown, comes into her first season at 6-14 months of age. The Italian greyhound, which will mature at around 7 pounds, will have her first season at approximately 18-24 months. The 55-pound Clumber spaniel may not have a first season until she is close to 24 months of age while the Cavalier King Charles Spaniel, with a mature weight of about 18 pounds will have her first season from about six to 14 months. There simply does not seem to be any rhyme or reason. There is a lot of variance breed to breed and, within each breed, from bitch to bitch. There does not seem to be a correlation between weight at maturity and the age of onset of puberty (the first season). About the only connection that you may see if you have a number of girls is what is called the "dormitory effect". It is common in human young women who are housed together to share monthly cycles and it is relatively common for bitches living in a "pack" situation to come into season around the same time.

If you have decided to breed your bitch, you can also expect many variables. Some bitches are ready for breeding by day 7 or so and others may not be ready until day 16. Old-time breeders made a practice of breeding their girls on days 9, 11 and 13 and those breeding practices make a lot of sense. They may not have had the scientific knowledge that we do, but they understood that breeding the bitch on those days created a litter. Bitches appear to ovulate on average about 9-10 days after the first signs of her season can be observed. The other factor that made those breedings successful was the long life span of the sperm. Knowing for a certainty that sperm live in the reproductive tract for as long as 5-7 days, and that eggs live at least 4-5 days, the overlap of long-lived sperm to viable egg was what made the days of 9, 11 and 13 successful.

The bitch drops her eggs when her progesterone level hits approximately five ng/ml. After she ovulates, the progesterone level will rise sharply, and start to drop after the eggs are either fertilized or dead. If they are fertilized, she will need to keep her progesterone level at about five through the nine weeks of gestation in order to stay in whelp. If you have had bitches who lost litters at around day 50, ask you vet to check the progesterone level on your bitch throughout her gestation. The vet can give you supplemental progesterone and instruct you in its use.

After the bitch has ovulated her eggs will take 2-3 days to ripen and live at least another 2 days after that. If she is bred two days prior to when she ovulates, the sperm will still be alive and well and able to fertilize the eggs when they have ripened. While doing progesterone levels, I have owned bitches that stood, flagged, and allowed a breeding 3 and even four days prior to ovulation. I have also owned a bitch who allowed a breeding 12 days after ovulation. (There were no puppies after that late breeding). After the eggs have dropped, the progesterone level continues to climb reaching as high as 80 ng/ml before it begins its decline. I have known a bitch that missed a breeding when her progesterone was 15 and I know a bitch that was bred a single time with a progesterone level of 21.6 who had six live pups. There does not seem to be a standard of how high the progesterone level can go while the eggs are ripe and still able to be fertilized.

What I am trying to tell you is that about the only numbers and facts that are firm and set in somewhat uncertain stone are these:

- Sperm is viable for at least five-seven full days, probably several days more
- Bitches ovulate (drop their eggs) when their progesterone level reaches 5 ng/ml
- The eggs live for around 4-5 days
- If timing is an issue… you simply _must_ know the day of ovulation for your bitch. If you are planning a breeding using chilled or frozen sperm, guesswork just will not do it. Only knowing the day of ovulation is going to facilitate a breeding that results in a litter.

If you are planning a breeding where the bitch needs to be shipped out, the sperm needs to be shipped in or if you are using either fresh chilled and extended sperm or frozen sperm, timing is critical. If you have kept careful records, you may have a good idea when your bitch is about ready to come into season. If you know the time is soon, but not yet there and you are planning to breed her this is the time to worm her one last time and make sure her immunizations are current if you are still vaccinating yearly. Many of us no longer do. You might want to consider a trip to the vet for a prenatal visit. The vet can check for strictures and discuss with you the general over all health of the bitch. Start watching her carefully at that time. If the boys seem to be particularly enthralled with her, she may well be starting into season. Boys will often know when a season is approaching before you see any signs of it. Once you see red blood (and sometimes it is not there… good luck on that one) count that as day one. By day five, you need to see your vet. The vet will probably first do a vaginal swab to look at the skin cells under the microscope. If there are many normal looking vaginal skin cells, the vet will know that the cornification process has not yet started or is just beginning. If the slide shows that cornification is well under way, the vet will want to draw blood for a progesterone test.

At the end of this chapter, I will discuss progesterone testing itself, but for the time being, we will just focus on the timing issues. There are tests that can be done in-house at the vet's office but they are not terribly accurate. If you are looking for accuracy, the blood sample will need to be sent out to an outside lab with results available the next day. Handling of the blood sample is critical, but there will be more about that later. Depending on those results, you will need to return for serial progesterone levels at times determined by your vet. The test results will often say something like: "The progesterone level is 3.6. The ideal day for breeding is tomorrow and the next day". However…if the progesterone level never hits five, it means that there are no eggs to fertilize so there is no ideal day for breeding. This happens more often than you would think. It certainly happens during what is called a "split season". In a split season, the bitch will exhibit some of the signs of being in season such as bleeding and swelling. Males will be attracted to her. She will not be likely to hump other females, they will not hump her and she will probably not ever welcome the advances of the stud dog, although a very few do. In a few days, or a couple of weeks, the season resumes and the eggs are released during the second half of the split season. Continue the progesterone testing as recommended by your vet until you know for a certainty that your bitch has ovulated. In addition, each bitch and each season will be different. Their schedule of ovulation does not always match what the lab has determined is appropriate timing. Even though it is expensive, if you are planning an important breeding, keep doing the progesterone tests until you know that the bitch has ovulated.

Once you know that the bitch has ovulated because her progesterone level has hit the level of five ng/ml, you can seriously get to the business of breeding. If you are planning a natural breeding, you can allow the bitch to be with the stud dog and he may well breed her. You can very accurately predict the day of whelping if you know the exact day that progesterone level reached five. Your litter will arrive on days 62-64 after the progesterone reached five. Most will arrive 63 days after the progesterone level reached five. <u>Puppies are born sixty-three days after their eggs are released.</u>

When is a litter due? When are they early? When are they late?

The day that the egg destined to become a puppy was released was day one of the gestation. NOT the day it was fertilized. NOT the day the bitch was bred. The puppy began its sixty-three journey toward birth on the day it was released as an egg. You will often hear breeders saying things like, "My litter was born on day 67." No, your litter was born on day 63. Your bitch was bred a few days before she ovulated, but your pups were born 63 days after they were released from the ovary. That is when the clock started. You will often hear, "My pups were premature. They were born on day 57." No, the litter was born on day 63 after ovulation. Your bitch was bred a few days after she ovulated. Let us see if I can explain this in a way that makes it clearer. Your bitch ovulated on 4 August. Her pups are due exactly 63 days later and that is when they will come. They will be born on 6 October. The stud dog bred her on August 1, three days before she ovulated. You start the clock on that day, and you are expecting pups on October 3 based on days of breeding. Remember though… we already know when the pups will arrive: they will arrive on October 6. When they arrive on October 6, you will say, "My pups were born late. They were born on day 66." Or maybe with that same bitch, same season, the stud dog bred her on August 8 and you base your figures on that day, add 63 days and figure the day of whelping as October 10. When the pups are born on schedule, October 6, you say, "My pups were born 4 days prematurely." No, they were born 63 days after they left the ovary.

Puppies start turning into puppies the day their eggs are released from the ovary. It takes them 63 days to turn from an egg into a puppy. The day of ovulation is the day their clocks start. Their clocks run for 62-64 days, but the figure is actually probably closer to 63. It is hard to pin point the day of ovulation even doing serial tests, so there is the variable of 24 hours one way or the other. When the bitch releases her eggs, she releases them all at once. There is not any of this release one or two on Monday, a couple on Tuesday and the rest on Wednesday. This is one of those "breeder" myths. When they have a pup that is significantly smaller than the others are, they will say it was fertilized last. Well, it may have been the very first one fertilized since fertilization takes place around the same time for every egg. What accounts for runts is not being fertilized later than the other eggs; it is their placement within the uterine horn. Every time a bitch has a litter, the placenta has been attached in a circle around the entire uterine horn as the baby wears its little "placenta belt". When the placenta comes off the wall of the uterus, it leaves behind some mild scarring. If another egg in the next litter happens to unluckily pick that same spot for implantation, that mild scarring may prevent the most advantageous implantation of the placenta and the puppy will be smaller because he simply did not receive as much nutrition as the other pups did. These are the things that are necessary to learn from this paragraph:

- The gestational puppy clock starts ticking the second the egg is released, not when the breeding takes place
- The gestational puppy clock ticks for 63 days and then the pup is born
- The eggs are all released at the same time
- Runts are not premature pups; they are pups who had a poor implantation site in the uterus
- Large pups are not overdue pups; they are pups who had a great implantation site in the uterus
- Pups are born 63 days after ovulation
- Pups are born 63 days after ovulation
- Pups are born 63 days after ovulation. Oops! Looks like I repeated myself a few times. Oh well, it bears repeating:
- Pups are born 63 days after ovulation.

Use of Fresh Chilled Extended Sperm and Frozen Sperm

Since I repeated myself in the previous paragraph, I do not want to make that same mistake twice. Refer back to the chapter on artificial insemination and the timing for chilled and frozen sperm will be explained fully.

By the time the progesterone level has reached 3.5 ng/ml or so, the bitch will allow other bitches to mount her. She may or may not allow males to mount her or breed her, but for sure, she will allow other bitches to mount. By the time her progesterone levels reach five, she will usually stand and flag. Most bitches will allow breeding at this time. Some stud dogs will happily breed a bitch that has just recently ovulated but some will be slightly more selective and wait until he can smell that the eggs are ripe. Once her eggs are ripe… the bitch will stand, flag, flirt, play bow, hump the other bitches past the point of all reason and in general, act like a bitch who needs to be bred. Instinct tells her that the biological clock is ticking on those eggs and she will be very intent upon getting them fertilized. By this time, there have been changes in the body of the bitch that also give us our signal that the time is perfect for breeding. These are the things that you will need to know about the bitch that has ovulated and has eggs ready for fertilization:

- Her progesterone level has reached or exceeded 5 ng/ml
- The vaginal discharge is usually light yellow by now. Sometimes still red or pink, but most of the time it is light yellow.

- The vulva is swollen and quite soft

- The vulva is no longer between her back legs, pointing downward. It has lifted and is now pointing more outward… in the direction from which the penis will be approaching.

- The odor coming from the bitch is strong.

- If you stroke the vulva, it will lift and "wink". The tail will "flag" or go off to the side to make room for the penis.

- If you insert a gloved finger into the vulva, you may feel, and even see a clasping movement of the vulva.

- If you introduce her to the stud dog, she will flirt, chase, play bow, and invite him to breed her by showing him her rear end.

- When she does these things…she is ready for breeding.

- Oh and one last thing I may have forgotten: Puppies are born 63 days after ovulation, just in case I did not say that before.

Progesterone Labs: Handle With Care

It is very important that the blood for progesterone levels be handled appropriately in order for the test results to be accurate. It is your responsibility, since you are paying for the test to make sure that the test is accurate to the best of everyone's ability.

This is how progesterone blood draws work. The blood is drawn into a tub called a Serum Separator tube (SST). The tube is pictured here. The SST contains a substance known as a barrier gel. The barrier gel is at the bottom of the tube when you first draw the blood into the tube. After the blood is collected, it is placed in a centrifuge and spun. It must be spun immediately instead of allowing it to clot.

The centrifuge spins at such a high rate of speed that it causes the blood to separate into two different components. The red blood cells and other solid particles are collected at the bottom of the tube and the clear yellow serum is collected at the top. The barrier gel rises to the middle of the tube and keeps the two blood components—the red blood cells and the clear yellow serum—from mixing again. It acts as a barrier between the two components. The part of the blood that contains the progesterone is the clear serum. Once the serum is separated, it should ideally be poured off into a transport tube and sent along without the solid particles or the barrier gel. The reason for this is that the progesterone in the serum will bind to the barrier gel. Over time, more and more progesterone will bind itself to the gel until there is very little progesterone left. By the time the SST has sat for 24 hours, there is not enough progesterone left to give a level that even approximates accuracy. Because progesterone binds to the barrier gel in the SST, the blood draw needs to be drawn early in the morning and taken to the lab as soon as possible so that the serum component can be removed from contact with the barrier gel. Once the serum is off the barrier gel, the progesterone is actually quite stable. Ask your vet about the timing for the tube of blood. Make sure that the progesterone level you get is as accurate as possible: *Draw blood, spin immediately, pour serum off the barrier gel into a transporter tube and take to lab.*

Notes:

7- Oxytocin, Calcium and Glucose

The Three Musketeers of Whelping

Three substances: oxytocin, calcium and glucose play an important role in the whelping process of the canine. They work hand in hand as a team in the coordination of the delivery of the puppies.

Oxytocin

Oxytocin is a complex little hormone that has three basic actions. It is a naturally occurring hormone manufactured in the hypothalamus gland and stored in the pituitary gland until needed by the bitch. It is synthetically produced and can be given as an injection as needed in the canine, although never in the human. In human OB, it is infused only by IV pump, slowly and steadily. It has several uses in the canine reproductive process. In order to understand exactly how oxytocin works, you first have to have a clear understanding of the way that muscles work in the mammal.

There are two types of muscle tissue: "striated muscle", which comprises all of the muscles in your body over which you have physical control. You can open and close your fingers: striated muscle. You can walk down the street: striated muscle. The other type of muscle tissue is called "smooth muscle". You have no control over these muscle fibers. You cannot make your uterus contract: smooth muscle. You cannot make your heart beat: Smooth muscle. Even lung and bronchial tissue is composed of smooth muscle. You breathe even while you are sleeping… smooth muscle. Oxytocin is a selective hormone, which causes the contractibility of the smooth muscle in only two locations, the uterus and the milk glands. (Terbutaline, a drug, causes the _relaxation_ of the uterus, heart and lungs.)

- Oxytocin is used to increase the quality of the contractions during labor by increasing frequency and duration.
- Oxytocin alters the cell membrane of the uterine cells so that calcium can enter the uterine cells during labor thus creating stronger and more effective contractions.
- Oxytocin is used as a clean out shot following delivery.
- Oxytocin is the hormone responsible for milk letdown and milk ejection during breast-feeding. As the puppies nurse, oxytocin is released naturally from the mother's pituitary gland, causing contraction of the breast tissue, allowing milk to be released to the pups.
- Oxytocin also causes mild uterine contractions causing the involution (return to pre-gestational size) of the uterus following delivery every time the puppies nurse for several days.

Oxytocin is produced synthetically and is used in human medicine under the name "Pitocin". It is widely utilized in human obstetrics as a medication to induce labor. It is very effective for induction in humans and in mares, but has not been found to be useful in cows, ewes, does or sows. It is not known if Oxytocin can induce normal labor in the full term bitch. **Do not attempt to use it to induce labor.**

Oxytocin during Labor

Oxytocin is used to facilitate a more effective labor during whelping. Oxytocin is responsible for the frequency and duration of the contractions. (The chapter on whelping will give you more information about this.) It is responsible for the timing of the contractions. By using your hand to feel the uterine muscle as it contracts, you can get a reliable idea of when the contractions are occurring and how long they are lasting. While oxytocin is a very, very useful drug, it is also a double-edged sword. It can also be very dangerous if administered inappropriately. Your vet is the very best resource to learn how to utilize oxytocin for a whelping experience that is safe for both mom and puppies.

If your bitch has been laboring for a while and has not delivered a pup, it may be time to do an intervention, particularly if she is pushing without results. If the contractions are irregular, short in duration and not resulting in the delivery of a puppy, you may want to consider using a dose of oxytocin on your girl. It is available only by prescription from your vet. You will need syringes/needles to administer it. Ask your vet to provide the oxytocin and follow his instructions on its use. Vets differ as to how they feel that oxytocin can be administered. Some favor larger doses given intramuscularly, and some recommend smaller doses given sub cutaneously. Follow the instructions of your vet when using oxytocin on the laboring bitch. Oxytocin is capable of creating a contraction, which can be strong enough and last long enough to squeeze off the oxygen supply to the puppies. It can kill a puppy. It can even create a contraction strong enough to cause the uterus to rupture. On the other hand, it can set up a contraction that is useful enough to deliver a puppy which otherwise would have died in utero. A double-edged sword for sure…*very useful but very dangerous.*

Oxytocin as a "Clean Out" Injection

Oxytocin is used in the canine whelping process as a "clean out" injection to create uterine contractions that will cause the expulsion of after-delivery tissues, blood and blood clots. Some recent studies have suggested that the use of oxytocin as a clean out shot is associated with prevention of mastitis in the bitch. Bitches that are given a clean out shot are much less likely to develop mastitis. Ask your vet to provide you with oxytocin prior to whelping time. If your vet does not feel that it is necessary, stress that you have read that it helps to prevent mastitis and that you would feel more comfortable if you had it on hand for clean out. Follow the vets' instruction on the use of oxytocin.

Oxytocin for Milk Ejection

As the puppies begin sucking on the dam's nipples, the pituitary gland will secrete small amounts of oxytocin to encourage the milk letdown reflex and cause the ejection of milk. The oxytocin also causes mild uterine contractions which will cause the involution (returning to the pre-gestational state) of the uterus and continue the clean out process. If your dam does not get milk for her puppies, consult with your vet about the possibility of giving her three very small "micro-doses" of oxytocin to encourage milk letdown. It is also a drug that is useful in encouraging maternal actions and behaviors when used in these very small doses.

In summary, oxytocin has several functions during the laboring, post delivery and nursing phase of canine reproduction:

- It cannot be used to induce labor in the canine.
- It is responsible for starting uterine contractions.
- It is responsible for cleaning out the uterine horns after whelping.
- It is responsible for triggering the milk letdown reflex and for milk ejection.
- It works hand in hand with calcium to create contractions of the right frequency, duration and strength.
- It alters the cell membrane so that calcium can enter the muscle cells.
- Can be useful for bringing milk in if mom's lactation reflex is slow.
- Can be useful to encourage maternal actions and behaviors in the bitch.
- Can be dangerous for both mom and puppies and should be used only as directed by your vet.

Glucose

Because the moms generally lose their appetites the day of delivery, and can subsequently go without a meal for several hours, it is a good idea to keep some Nutra Stat® on hand to make sure the glucose level stays up. It is probably not very common for the glucose level to drop, but giving the bitch in labor a little Nutra Stat® from time to time will certainly not hurt her or her puppies and it might well help them all. Nutra Stat® is a good quality product that moms like and will take without a problem. Offer your bitch a small amount of it on a spoon during labor from time to time and it will help her to keep her energy at a higher level and will get to the babies in utero. If a puppy has not been able to nurse from mom for the first two hours of its life, I always tube feed half the weight of the two-hour-old puppy in ounces in ccs of Pedialyte®. If a puppy weighs 6 oz, I tube feed the puppy 3 ccs of Pedialyte®. Usually, it is only necessary to do this one time and by that time, the puppy can go to mom's breast. If you need to repeat it, do it every 2-3 hours and change to a milk substitute such as Esbilac. This is done to keep the glucose level normal on the puppy. Once a puppy has been allowed time to latch on and nurse, the addition of Pedialyte® or Esbilac is not necessary.

Calcium

Calcium is critical in the role of delivery of the litter. Decades ago, it was almost unheard of for a bitch to have a c-section. Now c-sections are very common in many breeds. In some breeds, c-sections are almost at 100%. Part of the increase in c-sections is because breeders have selectively bred for certain anatomical features, like very large heads combined with very small pelvises. This has made c-sections necessary. The other reason that we see so many c-sections is because, in an effort to do everything we can do to insure healthy moms and healthy babies, we supplement our bitches with Calcium. Some of us do it by feeding a raw diet, some of us do it by giving them extra calcium tabs and some do it by increasing the intake of calcium rich foods during gestation. Many vets recommend that bitches in whelp should be on a diet of puppy kibble that is very high in calcium. During the days when bitches delivered naturally the vast majority of the time, breeders fed their dogs either a diet of table scraps, generic kibble or a combination of both because that was all they had. They did not supplement with calcium tabs because those products were simply not available to them.

Calcium is not about bones and teeth. That is what we always think of when we think the word "calcium", but that is not what it is all about. Calcium is all about *muscle contractibility*. That is the most important role it plays in our bodies. Television commercials encourage us to drink milk to keep our bones and teeth strong. It should also be telling us that we need calcium to keep our hearts beating, our leg muscles walking and our uterus contracting when necessary. The purpose of oxytocin is to determine the frequency and duration of uterine contractions. The purpose of calcium is to give strength and intensity to the contraction.

Oxytocin is responsible for frequency and duration of the contraction. It determines how often the uterus contracts and how long the contraction lasts. Calcium is responsible for creating strength of contractions. Calcium determines how strong the contractions are. The two substances are a team.

Calcium is stored primarily in our bones. The release of calcium into the blood stream is regulated by our parathyroid gland. When we need extra calcium the parathyroid gland goes to work, pulls it out of the bones, and puts it into the blood stream. The parathyroid gland is a lazy little thing and if someone else provides calcium on a day-to-day basis, Mr. Parathyroid just goes to sleep at the wheel so to speak. So, here we are… loading the bitch down with extra calcium every day so that those pups will have big strong bones and nice little white teeth. The parathyroid gland, which used to act as the gate keeper by pulling calcium out of the storage units in the body as it was needed has nothing much to do anymore, so it slacks off and no longer does much of anything. It forgets the job it has and takes a long vacation. The day comes when the uterus decides to contract strongly for several hours in its effort to push out the puppies and there is no gatekeeper to pull calcium from the bones to create good strong contractions. We made the job of the parathyroid gland obsolete by supplementing the bitch with calcium. With our good intentions, we put a perfectly good parathyroid gland out of a job.

Just to make it perfectly clear: you have supplemented your bitch with calcium if you have given her daily pet tabs. You have supplemented your bitch with calcium if you have put her on puppy food. You have supplemented your bitch with calcium if you have fed her calcium rich foods, such as ice cream, cheese and milk or other dairy products on a regular basis. You have supplemented your bitch with calcium if you have fed her a raw diet during gestation. All of that nice raw bone was just packed to the brim with calcium, and your bitches uterus was just a uterine inertia waiting to happen.

Once you have figured out that your bitch isn't contracting, pushing and delivering puppies as she should be, you may decide to give her some oxytocin to help her on her way. Guess what? It may very well not do any good. When you set the bitch up for failure by supplementing her diet with calcium, you also sabotaged her body's ability to utilize oxytocin as well. Oxytocin is the hormone that controls the rate of calcium that is allowed to enter the cells of the uterus. So you've supplemented the oxytocin, but what good does it do if the parathyroid gland is off in La-La land? Instead of acting as the gatekeeper by pulling calcium out of the bones and sending it into the blood stream, the parathyroid gland has gone to sleep. There is no extra calcium being sent into the blood stream. The oxytocin is there to open the door (actually the cell membrane) and allow calcium to enter the cell and get to work on those contractions but where is the calcium?

Calsorb®

Lucky for breeders, there is a product containing calcium that is safe to use, easy to obtain and relatively inexpensive. The product is called Calsorb®. It is a clear gel product packaged in a syringe to be given orally. If the bitch has been pushing for a while and nothing seems to be happening, you can administer three mls of Calsorb® by mouth and it will strengthen the contractions. It isn't at all unusual to give Calsorb® and see a puppy delivered within 10 minutes or so. Calsorb® is a wonderful product, not just because of its effectiveness, but because of its safety. It doesn't have the side effects of oxytocin and is safe for mom and babies.

Before you use Calsorb®, count the heartbeats of the bitch. Keep a record of her normal heart rate. An adult dogs' heart rate should be about 130-150 beats per minute. After giving a couple of doses of Calsorb®, check her heart rate again. If you notice a change in heart rate over 15 beats per minute or a change in the normal rhythm of the heart, discontinue the Calsorb®. These changes are rare with Calsorb® but worth mentioning and monitoring. Bitches will often throw up after taking Calsorb.

A Whelping Analogy

I would like you to be able to clearly visualize the interdependent role of each of the three chemical components of whelping: glucose, oxytocin and calcium. I want you to imagine this team of three musketeers for a moment. They have been assigned a job of great importance. The job requires intricate teamwork and three primary skills. Glucose's skill is to provide energy and endurance to the team endeavor. Without the energy that Glucose provides, the other two musketeers won't have the energy needed to work. Oxytocin's skill is to regulate timing and rhythm so that things move forward as they should. If it is not present, nothing can start, nothing can move forward. Oxytocin also opens the door so that Calcium can enter the cells. Calcium brings the skill of brute strength to the task. If calcium is missing, the job cannot be accomplished because the other two are too weak to function without that assistance. If any one of the musketeers is missing, the other two are unable to complete the task for which they are responsible. The three musketeers of whelping: oxytocin, calcium and glucose will come to the rescue for you many times in your careers as breeders. Keep them close and treat them with respect. View them as a team working together to whelp your puppies. If you have seen to the needs of Glucose and Calcium by correct diet and nutrition, the bitch's body will usually see to the needs of oxytocin.

Notes:

| |
| |
| |
| |
| |
| |
| |
| |
| |
| |

8- Whelping

Sometimes Natural, Sometimes a Nightmare

The biggest difference between assisting a human mom to deliver her baby and assisting a canine mom to deliver hers is that the human mom can talk to you. Mrs. Hannah Human can tell you all kinds of things that Ms. Daisy Doggie cannot. A human patient can tell you when her contractions started, where the pain is located, how strong the contractions are and how long they are lasting. She can tell you how her last delivery went as well. By taking her blood pressure and other vital signs, you can gather even more information. Add into that pool of data the fact that the patient's OB/GYN has sent you a history of the patient's last 8 months or so and you can really begin to get a good solid picture of your patient. Once she is in your department, you can place fetal monitors and perform vaginal exams and you would be surprised at how much useful information is yours by then.

In today's modern OB practice, it isn't uncommon to know the approximate size of the infant, the gender, the comparative size of the baby's head versus the size of the mother's pelvis, and the gestational age of the baby, both by dates of conception and development of the fetus as determined by ultrasound before the patient ever shows up at the labor/delivery department. Additionally, you may have knowledge of many of the risk factors that the mother's state of health has created. Once mom has presented in the department and you have placed a fetal monitor, you will know the timing of the contractions and the baby's heart rate. Interestingly enough, the baby's heart rate doesn't really present much information about the heart itself, but gives us a lot of information about the neurological status of the baby. A vaginal exam will tell you if the baby is head down, or breech, the status of the cervix and where the baby is in the birth canal.

I still long for all that good information every time I whelp a litter. There are other pieces of information that our bitches will give us that are also reliable to assist us in whelping. Fetal monitors that were made for human monitoring are now being used on bitches in labor. If you feel that this technology is useful to you, then I would encourage you to pursue it. However, one of the great myths that circulate both in human medicine and in canine medicine is that a fetal monitor can detect the STRENGTH of the contraction. They are absolutely, unequivocally, NOT able to determine the strength of the contractions. They are able only to tell you the frequency: how often the contractions are occurring, and the duration: how long the contractions are lasting. Click on the link below and read it carefully. http://babies.sutterhealth.org/laboranddelivery/ld_fam.html You will be able to read that an external fetal monitor is unable to determine the strength of the contraction. Alternatively, read: "Fetal Heart Monitoring Principles and Practices", which is distributed by AWHONN and written by Feinstein, Torgersen and Atterbury, published by Kendall/Hunt.

There are Internal Pressure Catheters for use in human medicine that do allow us to determine the strength of the contraction, but these aren't available for dogs, nor would they be useful on an animal with two uterine horns. Human technology is designed for one uterus, and one infant. In labor/delivery if we had a mother who was pregnant with twins, or triplets, each fetus had its own fetal monitor. It is difficult, if not impossible, to translate technology designed for one uterus and one fetus to another mammal with two uterine horns and several fetuses.

No matter what anyone tells you and no matter what you may have read: A fetal monitor placed on the abdomen cannot tell you how strong or how effective a contraction is. It cannot determine if the puppy is not well positioned for delivery. It cannot tell you if the contractions are strong enough to expel the baby, not with canines and not with humans. Do not be surprised if your vet also believes that a fetal monitor can determine the strength or intensity of a contraction. Unless your vet has worked extensively with fetal monitors in a labor/delivery setting, they would not have the knowledge base necessary to know their limitations. The tracing made by an external monitor can "look" as though the contractions are very, very strong and the mother can be sleeping through them. On the other hand, they can look like tiny little anthills during the actual delivery of the infant. External fetal monitors absolutely cannot determine the strength of the contractions. Your fingertips can do a better job by palpating the uterus during the contractions.

The Natural and Uncomplicated Whelping

Even though our bitches cannot give us a lot of verbal information, their bodies and their behaviors can tell us a lot about their laboring procedures. Of course, there will be variables from bitch to bitch, and whelping to whelping, but I would like to describe to you the "ideal" whelping scenario. Later on, we'll get into those situations that are nightmarish. Right now, let's just talk about a whelping that is textbook perfect.

Because you have been taking the temperatures of your bitch and keeping a record, you have already figured out that delivery is due within the next 24 hours or so and you are prepared. The whelping box is ready for the mom, and warming box is ready for the puppies. You are prepared. That is the first component of the textbook perfect whelping—your own preparation. The most ideal whelping in the

54

world can feel pretty awful if you've planned a dinner party for that day, you don't have any supplies on hand, and you haven't arranged a set up for mom and babies.

The bitch may not eat the day of whelping. That may be your first tell tale sign. She may refuse her meals. She will still be drinking water, but she is refusing her food. I've had girls who will quite happily eat ice cream during contractions though, so loss of appetite is just one more variable. It happens more often than not, however, so you can watch for that sign. Several hours prior to the actual delivery, she will start having contractions. Her contractions will start out being rather mild in intensity, short in duration and irregular. These contractions are causing her cervix to open and thin. She knows what is happening. Always be aware that even a maiden bitch knows she is getting ready to have puppies. Do not suppose that they are in the dark about the fact that they are in whelp. They are not. They are filled with instinct, and they are well aware of what is happening to them. They have felt puppies kicking them for weeks. They know. Because they know they are about ready to have a litter of puppies, they will absolutely want you to be near them. They will begin to be restless. Your bitch will bark at you and bark at you again until you stop what you are doing and listen to her. When she is in labor, she will want the people who are dear to her….near to her. If you think she was clingy before, wait until you see how she acts when she is in labor. She will not want to let you out of her sight, and if she is dependent and close to more than one family member, she will insist that everyone be present. She will become agitated if her people are not nearby.

The bitch in labor will have a very strong urge to dig and nest. She will start this behavior about a week or more before the actual whelping date, but when she is in active labor, it will become much more pronounced, more frequent and much lengthier. She will dig. She will dig in closets, laundry baskets, her toy box, in her whelping box and on your bed. Wherever she is, she will be seeking a place to dig. It is best to have her in a controlled environment because she will seek out places that are inaccessible to you, such as behind your TV unless you watch her carefully. Give her a large cardboard box filled with old washcloths and hand towels and you will save yourself a lot of grief. If she is given a specific place in which to dig, she will often use it and avoid shredding the carpet in your closet. You can either use the whelping box for this by adding several fun things for her to dig into or use a separate box if she prefers it. Offer her a nice cloth filled location for her digging.

She will pant. The panting starts about the same time that the laboring process begins and is very pronounced. It isn't a function of being hot or cold. It is simply a function of the laboring process in the canine. Don't worry about it. Once she has her first puppy, the panting usually stops completely. It seems that the panting is only a part of the whelping of the first puppy. Once she delivers a puppy, the puppy will become her focal point and she will become less agitated, less clingy, and less likely to be in constant motion. Make sure that you give her access to water all during the laboring process. All that panting will make her mouth very dry. They like spray bottles at this time. Spray water into her mouth if she enjoys it. Give her small bites of glucose rich food at this time.

She will be in a state of constant motion. The bitch in labor doesn't usually lay quietly in the whelping box. She is agitated, nervous; her heart rate is elevated, probably due to all that panting. She may circle repeatedly. She will try to lick her vulva. At this time, she is still only contracting. She hasn't yet begun the pushing process. The picture that you are going to be looking at in the bitch in labor is this: Very dependent and seeking your physical presence, agitated and nervous, panting, and in motion: digging, turning in circles during contractions, and pacing between contractions. Once the cervix has thinned and is open, she will begin the pushing process. This first stage of labor may last for several hours. This is normal. If she appears to tire, give her oxygen using the "blow by" method.

Do not expect the bitches pushing behaviors to mirror those of the human delivery. We have all either delivered babies, been present during the delivery of babies, or watched human deliveries on TV and movies. We have watched it from start to finish. Remember the labor delivery nurse counting to 10 while the human patient bears down and pushes? This won't happen when your bitch delivers her babies. First off, they can't count, so they won't cooperate when you try to count while they push. Secondly, their pushing is done in very short little doses. They may push for 2-3 seconds at a time. Usually, they will be in a sitting position with their heads extending upwards while they give short little pushes as they push the baby from the uterine horn into the birth canal. Often, you will know when the puppy has entered the birth canal because the bag of water will precede the puppy by several minutes.

The bag of water may be ballooning out from the vulva (see picture at right). The bag of water is your signal that there is a puppy in the birth canal. It will usually be filled with green tinged fluid. Although this is a sign of fetal distress in a human delivery, it is normal for the canine delivery. Anything of any shade of green is bad news when it is a human baby, but it is completely normal in the canine. Don't give it a thought. Don't break it, don't touch it. Let

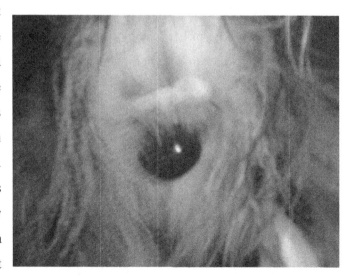

mom take care of it on her own. She may reach back and lick it causing it to break. She may ignore it and keep pushing. Both are normal.

Once the puppy is in the birth canal, the bitch will usually stand on all four legs, lift her tail, hunch her back and push with more force for a longer period. She may extend her head upwards. As the puppy approaches the opening of the vulva, the area will swell, extend slightly and push forward. This is just the body of the puppy pushing against the soft tissues of the vulva. It is a sign that everything is going as it should. The puppy may be born feet first or head first. Both are common in the whelping of puppies. Being born feet first is not a sign of problems in the whelping process. About 40% of all pups are born feet first. The puppy may or may not be born enclosed in its little sac. If the puppy is born inside the sack, you can quickly assist mom in tearing open the sack so that the puppy can begin breathing. The sac has two layers, be sure to open them both. Moms usually do a pretty good job of this, but you can certainly observe and help if necessary. If the puppy is born inside the sack, generally, it will come with the placenta as well and everything will come out together. This is normal. Sometimes, the puppy will come out of the vulva without its membranous sack and without its placenta. This is also normal. You can help at this point by grasping the puppy gently using a washcloth to give you traction (they are slippery little things). Hold the puppy as the placenta is delivered. Don't tug. Just support the baby as the next contractions push the placenta forward. Sometimes the body of the puppy will be out, but very close to the vulva, mom will be circling and perhaps licking the area. All is normal. Once the puppy is born, Mom will continue to lick, turn and even lift the puppy by its cord as she stimulates it to breathe. She will chew the cord through, crushing the blood vessels as she does so to prevent bleeding from the cord stump. At some point following delivery, put some Betadyne® on the cord stump. Following the delivery of the first puppy, mom will usually settle down and tend her baby until shortly before the delivery of the next puppy. When a puppy nurses from the mom, it stimulates uterine contractions which is useful. If only all our deliveries were textbook whelpings. Unfortunately, they are not, and it's time to move on to the next topic:

Sometimes Whelping is a Nightmare

I wish I could tell you that by reading this chapter, you will never have whelping problems again. I wish I could tell ME that by reading this chapter, I will never have whelping problems again. Unfortunately, we are all subject to the same difficulties when whelping our puppies. All that I can do is to describe the problems, tell you what might have caused them and give you suggestions as to what solutions might "fix" the problem. Most importantly of all, maybe I can help you to prevent some of the issues that I have encountered. If the solutions described here don't work, you are going to be in the same position that I have been in… driving to the emergency vet in the middle of the night for a c-section. Believe me; I have had my fair share of whelping nightmares. They have taught me a lot and it is because of those terrifying events that I feel qualified to discuss whelping with you. The textbook picture perfect whelping didn't scare me to the point where I was driven to learn all I could possibly learn. It was the dead puppy half in and half out during the entire trip to the emergency clinic that drove me to read, research and learn. It was prematurity, missed breedings and repeated c-sections that drove me to learn. Maybe I can help you to learn some things and I am sure I can learn from each of you. One of the things that is very frightening to me is that, just as in human medicine, the advent of fetal and uterine monitoring created only one thing: an increase in c-sections. I fear that in canine medicine it will do the same. Fetal monitoring has not been able to prevent most of the problems in the neonate that have always been there. The majority of the time when a baby looked simply awful on a monitor, it came out of its emergency c-section looking great. Information is being widely spread that you can use human fetal monitors to determine whether the contractions are strong enough to expel a puppy. **WRONG.** Information is also being given that you can detect fetal distress in a litter of puppies by use of a hand-held Doppler or a stethoscope. **WRONG.** I hope that by the time you have finished reading this book, you will know the limitations of human fetal monitoring when used with litters of puppies and you will be less likely to panic when natural and normal things are occurring.

Well before your bitch is ready to whelp, prepare yourself for an emergency. Here are some things that you can have nearby to be prepared to help your bitch should you run into difficulties. First of all, read this book. Read other resources as necessary until you have a well-grounded understanding of the entire whelping process. Next, get your supplies together. Discuss whelping with your vet. Ask questions. Ask the vet about the use of Oxytocin. If the vet agrees that you may have a need for it, get instructions for the use of this important, but very dangerous hormone during whelping. Because oxytocin is a dangerous drug, it is better that your veterinarian help you to understand its administration and dosages. Here is a list of supplies that you will need to be prepared for the whelping that may present problems.

- You will need a warmed box for your puppies. You can get instructions for the construction of this box from the book: <u>Puppy Intensive Care</u> or you can buy one directly from me. If you have whelping problems, you will need a safe place for your puppies while you tend to mom.
- You will need oxytocin and syringes with needles, as well as clear instructions from your vet as to dosage and mode of administration.
- Calsorb® and a stethoscope to check mom's heart rate.
- Oxygen and a regulator with tubing. (Refer to <u>Puppy Intensive Care</u> for instructions.) Oxygen is synonymous with strength and endurance. Giving it to a laboring bitch that is fatigued will give her strength and increase the oxygen available to the pups in utero. It will protect your bitch and it can save your puppies. Turn the oxygen to 2 liters per minute and hold the end of the tubing near her mouth and nose.

- Large tube of K-Y Jelly®, 20 cc syringe with a luer slip tip and a size 8 French Feeding tube.

- Plenty of warmed wash clothes.

- Latex gloves with a good firm fit for your hand and Betadyne® solution

- NutraStat ® or another sweetened product that your bitch will eat in small quantities from time to time while in labor. (Ice cream, Pediatlyte, honey....whatever your bitch prefers.)

- Rectal thermometer. Mom's rectal temperature will drop to an average of about 98.6 degrees Fahrenheit somewhere between 8-24 hours prior to whelping. This drop in temperature is thought to coincide with a sharp drop in progesterone levels. A rise in maternal temperature during labor of over 103.5 should be reported to your vet, as it could be a sign of infection. Whatever has caused this temperature increase may be infecting the babies as well. As soon as whelping is complete, notify your vet of the temperature increase.

- Keep on hand a good oral antibiotic such as Keflex or Baytril®. In the event of an infection, you can start the bitch on it until you can get to the vet.

Now for some basic information about whelping. I am going to dispense with scientific terminology when possible because I believe that when information is imparted in every day layman's terms, we learn it faster and we remember it longer. The three stages of labor for a bitch approximate the three stages of labor in a human. (The third stage is the expulsion of the placenta.)

Stage One

The first stage of labor is the time during which she will fail to eat her meals, be restless and anxious, pant continually, dig and want you near by. She may throw up, but most don't. If she does, don't worry. Human moms do it too, and I suspect it is just a reaction to the pain they feel. During this first stage, the cervix is thinning and opening. This stage lasts from 4 hours to about 12, but it can extend to 24. As long as you aren't seeing green discharge, you will know that none of the placentas have separated and things are fine. If she isn't pushing, you will know she is still in stage one. If you get lucky, stage one will begin around 7 am, and deliveries will be completed by 7 pm, but instead, they seem to want to start into stage one at 10 pm, keep you awake all night and deliver early in the morning. In human deliveries, stage one is shorter with subsequent deliveries. In the canine, stage one appears to last about the same length of time with each whelping. If your bitch has exhibited all of the stages of stage one, but she never produces a puppy, she is experiencing Primary Uterine Inertia.

Primary Uterine Inertia

Primary uterine inertia means that the bitch has exhibited the behaviors of a normal stage one labor, but she never pushes and she never delivers a puppy. (*contractions, no push, no pup*) There are several possible causes of primary uterine inertia:

- Some breeds have a genetic pre-disposition to primary inertia.
- Some specific bitches have a genetic pre-disposition to primary uterine inertia.
- Litters containing only one or two puppies can cause primary uterine inertia. Whatever it is that stimulates the labor to begin and finish is sometimes lacking or inadequate to finish the job when only one or two puppies are in the uterus.
- Conversely, litters that are too large also cause primary inertia. The uterus is stretched so much by the presence of too many puppies that the muscle fibers are too thin to contract efficiently.
- Not enough calcium present to create strong enough contractions to expel a puppy. Remember the three musketeers of whelping?
- Obesity in the bitch
- Illness or infection in the bitch

If the bitch has failed to respond to oxytocin and calcium, you need to take her to your vet. Obviously some of the causes of primary uterine inertia can't be "fixed". A c-section will be necessary to save the puppies. Some causes could have been prevented and some can be helped along by the addition of oxytocin and calcium. Primary uterine inertia is this: *Labor, no pushing, no puppy.*

Stage Two

Stage two of labor is the time when the puppies are moving from the uterine horn into the birth canal and out into the world. The birth canal is the cervix, the vagina and the vulva. As the puppy passes through the cervix, the cervical stretching causes a natural "pushing" reflex. The mom will begin her short little pushes as the baby passes through the cervix. Once the puppy has reached the vulva and those tissues have begun to bow outwards, the mom will often, but not always, stand up on all fours, lift her tail, hunch her back and push harder and for longer periods. At the first push, you will know that the bitch has entered into the second stage of labor. I did a lot of research on this topic and it didn't all give me the exact same information so I am going to go with the general idea and the average time span that was given: If your bitch has pushed for two hours without a puppy, you are very most likely looking at secondary uterine inertia. After one hour of pushing without a puppy, you should call your vet and let them know that you have a potential problem. Describe what you are seeing and what steps you have taken to improve the quality of the labor. The vet will appreciate the heads up so that the office schedule can be adjusted if need be. After two hours of pushing, you need to take your bitch to the vet. She is suffering from secondary uterine inertia and dystocia: *Contractions, pushing, no puppy.*

She may have passed through stage one of the laboring process and may even have delivered some of the puppies, but she has reached a point where she has pushed for one-two hours without a puppy. This is now called "dystocia". The puppy simply can't get out. Fetal dystocia reminds me of that old song lyric: "You keep a knockin' but you can't come in". Well, fetal dystocia is sort of like that song except the lyric should be: "You keep a knockin' but you can't get out". Sometimes you can reach a gloved finger (rinsed with Betadyne®) up into the birth canal and feel the puppy. Often, you can see the puppy's feet, nose, or even the entire head or half the body… but it is stuck. It can't get out. Welcome to the hell known as Secondary Uterine Inertia and Dystocia, and it really can be hell because you can witness the death of your puppy if you cannot get the puppy out. Sometimes secondary uterine inertia and dystocia are caused on the mother's end of the delivery and sometimes on the baby's end of it. Here are some of the maternal causes of dystocia:

- Genetic pre-disposition (can be any bitch)
- Genetic pre-disposition in specific breeds, some terriers and the breeds with large heads and small pelvis size.
- Immaturity, bitch too young to be having puppies
- Previous injury to the bitch
- Nutritional status
- Obesity
- Calcium Deficiency (Hmm, remember all those calcium supplements and the musketeers?)
- Vaginal strictures

Sometimes the babies are the guilty little guys and it is all their fault that they are stuck and can't get out. Here are some of the fetal causes of secondary uterine inertia and dystocia:

- Litter too large
- Litter too small
- Puppy too large
- Hydrocephalus (water on the brain has caused the head to be too large)

- Abnormal presentation: transverse (sideways), neck flexion (nose tucked into the chest instead of nose first. There are others, but the result is the same.
- Two puppies trying to come down the chute at once. (A variation on the song lyric: "I hear you a knockin' but you both can't come out.")
- Breech (rear end first with legs folded up toward the chest)
- CPD: Cephalopelvic disproportion: puppy's head too large for mom's pelvis, can occasionally happen in any breed and in any litter, but more likely in breeds with large heads and small pelvic size.

We've established that the bitch has either primary or secondary inertia. The uterus either isn't contracting often enough or hard enough or both and we know that we have fetal dystocia. We know the baby is there, but it can't get out. What do you do?

1) Administer Calsorb® orally. Three to four mls every half an hour or so as long as mom's heart rate and rhythm are normal. Heart rate should be 130-150 or so and regular with no skipping beats.

2) Administer oxytocin by either an injection into the muscle of the back rear leg (IM) or sub cutaneously under the skin around the neck and shoulders (SQ). Oxytocin has a half-life of a couple of minutes but even so, it is critically important not to exceed the recommended dose. Too much oxytocin can cause uterine tetany (contraction that doesn't end) or fetal distress by the continual squeezing of the placenta that will cut off oxygen to the baby's brain.

3) If you can reach a puppy part and you feel you can apply some traction to remove the puppy safely,

you can try this: Open a 20 cc syringe. Pull the plunger part completely out of the syringe. Fill the syringe with K-Y Jelly®. Reinsert the plunger part of the syringe and attach a size 8 French feeding tube to the end of the syringe. Gently thread the feeding tube up the vagina until you are behind the puppy. Push the plunger and insert all of the K-Y Jelly® into the vagina, hopefully BEHIND the puppy. Hold the bitch up on her back legs for about 30 seconds to allow the

K-Y Jelly® to start down the birth canal. After this brief period, stand her with her rear end facing you and an assistant holding her head. Then, using a washcloth or 4X4 gauze pads to give you traction, lift

the puppy UPWARD to lift it over the pelvic bones. If the puppy is alive and the head is out, you can be giving it oxygen during this entire procedure. The puppy pictured was breathing and you can see by the color of the tongue that he pinked up.

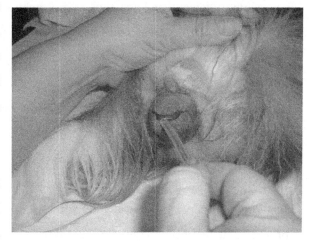

4) If I lived a good distance from a vet, I would ask my vet to teach me about episiotomies and I would attempt one if it mean the difference of a dead puppy or a living puppy. This is an extremely drastic and invasive measure, but if you are unable to get help for your bitch, it is an option provided you have discussed it thoughtfully with your vet.

5) Walk your bitch. Often walking will increase the quality and quantity of uterine contractions.

6) Gently massage the uterus. GENTLY, using no more pressure than you would if you were giving a newborn baby a back massage. Massaging the uterus will always create a contraction. If oxytocin is present and calcium levels are appropriate, massaging the uterus will set up a series of useful contractions. Remember: no harder than if you were massaging the back of a newborn baby.

7) Using a gloved finger rinsed with Betadyne®, reach into the vulva of the bitch and rub her vagina, particularly around the area of the spine. If you can reach her public bones, reach your finger over them and very gently pull them toward you. This will also stimulate a very, very strong contraction in a bitch. Stroke the top of the birth canal. This is called "feathering".

Keep in constant contact with your vet. The vet will appreciate being kept informed about what is happening and can give you instructions and suggestions for solutions. Relate which of the seven things listed above you have tried. Describe the response you have gotten. He will know that if you haven't gotten a response to those things, the office staff will need to be prepared for the emergency c-section that may be on the way. The vet will tell you when it is time to go in after the puppies. It is primarily a timing issue with bitches, and not a matter of fetal distress. This is as good a place as any to discuss fetal distress with you. Myths and misconceptions abound about this topic. It is necessary to have a very full and correct understanding of fetal monitoring before you utilize those techniques.

With the advent of fetal monitoring came the term fetal distress. True fetal distress is next to impossible to detect using a stethoscope or even using a hand-held Doppler. A decrease in fetal heart rate alone is not always a sign of fetal distress. In fact it rarely is. The next sections describe the things that can cause a decrease in fetal heart rate.

Variable Decelerations of Fetal Heart Tones: Ho Hum

If the umbilical cord is compressed during the contractions, the fetal heart rate will drop dramatically. It comes right back up and is not a sign of fetal distress. These drops in fetal heart tones are called variable decelerations and they are relatively harmless. They are not subtle, they are drastic. Usually changing mom's position for a while will make them go away. Very common, very normal, no reason for alarm. If by chance you hear these during a contraction, walk mom, turn her to another side, and hold her with her legs in the air for a couple of minutes… just think: slight reposition of the babies.

Early Decelerations of Fetal Heart Tones: Even MORE Ho Hum

As the contraction squeezes on the baby's head, the fetal heart tones will decrease. This sort of a deceleration will mirror the uterine contraction as viewed on a monitor. The deceleration will start when the contraction starts and end when the contraction ends. Very normal. Very harmless. No reason for alarm.

Late Decelerations of Fetal Heart Tones: NOW we're talkin' genuine fetal distress.

The only kind of deceleration of fetal heart tones that is considered dangerous to the fetus is the kind caused by squeezing of the placenta during the contraction. If the placenta is compressed too hard for too long, the baby's brain becomes oxygen deprived and the fetal heart rate will decrease. This decrease will begin to happen shortly AFTER the contraction has started. These decelerations of fetal heart tones end several seconds after the contraction has ended. The decrease is usually much too subtle to catch with a stethoscope or a Doppler, particularly when you are listening to the hearts of several babies at once. I would consider it an impossible task. Sometimes it is even too subtle to see on the monitor strip without quite a lot of experience reading and interpreting fetal monitor strips. You simply cannot make important judgments based on the rate of fetal heart tones on a litter of puppies. This human science isn't necessarily applicable to the canine. It simply doesn't translate well from human use to dog use. Without a fetal monitor for each puppy, and a monitor strip that we can read and interpret… we can't really and truly diagnose fetal distress in a litter of puppies. Knowing as much as I do, and having worked for 20 years in labor/delivery, I know that I am unable to do it. I doubt seriously that anyone can.

Several complications can happen following whelping. I only want to address three of the most common. They are all considered life threatening and all are fairly common. The first one is metritis.

Metritis

Although the vagina and vulva are usually filled with bacteria of one sort or another, the uterus is usually clean. The cervix is closed and offers protection to the interior of the uterus. During the birth process, the cervix is open and bacteria that are present can enter the uterus. Vaginal exams without the benefit of a gloved finger, rinsed with Betadyne® can also introduce bacteria into an otherwise clean environment. If bacteria, parts of placentas, or dead puppies are left behind, a serious infection can occur in your bitch. The signs and symptoms of metritis are as follows:

- Listlessness
- Loss of appetite
- Increased temperature, over 103.5 degrees Fahrenheit
- Odor. Again, an infection smells like raw meat that has gone bad. All body fluids have an odor, but infected tissue has an unmistakable smell. Once you have smelled it, you won't forget it. Call your vet immediately.
- Persistent vaginal discharge which may be bloody looking or yellow, but smells awful.

Mastitis

Mastitis is an infection of the breast. It may affect only one of the milk glands, or it may spread to several. The use of a clean out shot of oxytocin is associated with a decrease in the incidence of mastitis, so the clean out shot is well worth pursuing. The breast tissue may be swollen, warm to the touch, reddened… even almost purple looking. She may be refusing to allow her pups to nurse and because she is ill, she may ignore them completely. Here are the signs to watch for in mastitis:

- Lethargy, listlessness
- Loss of appetite
- Fever
- Refusal to allow the pups to nurse
- Warm, red, tender, swollen breast tissue

Your vet will treat with antibiotics, and if mastitis is severe enough, the involved breast tissue may require removal. Once your bitch is on antibiotics, give her a small amount of plain, live-cultured yogurt every day and give a little to the pups as soon as they are able to nurse. The antibiotic will kill off some of the normal bacteria in the intestines and the yogurt can help to replace them. Mastitis is a serious, life-threatening event. Contact your vet at the first sign. Check your post partum bitch every day. Look at her normal vaginal discharge and check her breasts. Stay on top of things.

Eclampsia

Eclampsia used to be called "milk fever". It is caused by low calcium levels. The word eclampsia means "seizure". As the mother's body manufactures milk and the puppies nurse almost continually, her normal calcium levels can become depleted. Although it isn't advisable to supplement with calcium BEFORE whelping, it is a very good idea to supplement with calcium AFTER whelping. You can do this with any good calcium supplement and with food products. I give my nursing bitches regular old American cheese every day. You can use Tums®, Pet Tabs, cottage cheese or something else that your vet recommends. You can switch mom to puppy kibble while she is nursing to add calcium to her diet. Eclampsia is very dramatic in its onset. It is almost as though you checked in on your bitch one minute and the next minute she was in full-blown eclampsia. Although it can happen at any time, it is most common during the first six weeks following delivery. It doesn't seem to matter how large the litter is, a bitch can still get eclampsia. My bitch with eclampsia had only two pups that were already five weeks old and supplementing their nursing with puppy kibble. The puppies' demand for milk will deplete the maternal supplies of calcium and eclampsia will occur. Make no mistake about it: eclampsia is a full-on medical emergency and it can kill your bitch quickly. Metritis and Mastitis, while serious, will have a slower onset. Eclampsia can happen within an hour and it can quickly progress to maternal death. Here are the symptoms of eclampsia:

- Extreme restlessness
- Rapid heart rate… too fast to count
- Panting, continual and hard
- Temperature… 106-107 isn't uncommon.
- Pacing nervously, but this will soon turn to staggering.
- It is hard to describe this, but if you put your hands on your bitch, you can feel the muscles underneath the skin twitching. Before the bitch progresses to seizures, you are able to feel the muscles twitching under the skin, and see it around the eyes and mouth. Remember what we discussed before about calcium being all about muscle contractibility? Well, a depletion of calcium will cause muscle seizures. Nothing works right in the absence of calcium.
- She will ignore her puppies. She is much too ill to care.

66

If you see these signs and symptoms in your bitch, you do not have time to waste. Immediately give her 6 ml of Calsorb® by mouth. Immediately use cool clothes on her abdomen where you can lay the cool clothes on bare skin. Wet her fur a little bit and go immediately to the vet if possible.

Notes:

9- Cesarean Sections

A Zipper Would Be More Convenient

There are two types of c-sections: planned and emergency. Both of them are performed the same way, using the same general techniques and instruments but the outcome for each is often different. Going into a planned c-section, the bitch is rested, the puppies are intact with their placentas in place and the outcome is frequently a positive one resulting in live puppies and a bitch who will recover quickly. Just as in human medicine, there are valid reasons for planning a scheduled c-section and a different set of reasons for having to resort to a c-section when the bitch is unable to whelp her litter. Some breeds are routinely scheduled for c-sections, particularly the breeds that have large heads and small pelvis areas, such as Bulldogs or Boston Terriers. In human medicine, that is called cephalo-pelvic disproportion, or CPD. What it means is that the head is too large to pass through the pelvis. This would be considered a valid reason for a scheduled c-section regardless of the breed of dog. This can be determined by having an x-ray done of your bitch a few days prior to her whelping date.

Your vet might also recommend planning a c-section if your bitch has an unusually large litter for the breed, a stricture that is not resolving under the influence of the normal hormones found in the pregnant bitch, or a known and documented history of litters lost during the whelping process. Even if you and your veterinarian have planned a c-section, you may be given instructions to allow the bitch to begin the laboring process before coming in for the surgery. First time moms may require some labor to allow the normal "hormone shower" to occur. This will help to prepare your bitch for motherhood and insure that her parenting skills are triggered. Follow the instructions of your vet as to the timing of the surgery.

Avoid utilizing vets who routinely recommend spaying a bitch during a c-section. A reproduction specialist or a breeder vet will recognize that each of your bitches is of great importance to you in your breeding programs and will assist you in the breeding and delivery of these valuable girls. Unless there is a specific need to do so, such as a ruptured uterus, do not agree to a spay during a c-section even if you know it is to be the last litter that your bitch may be having. The risk of bleeding increases significantly if a bitch is spayed during a c-section. The cost for spaying later is relatively inexpensive and the life of your bitch is worth much, much more. Do not place her in a position of unnecessary risk for excessive bleeding unless you have no other option. The removal of the uterus at the time of the c-section does not have an affect on the production of milk, nor does a single c-section mean that your bitch will have to have repeat c-sections in the future. Most reproduction vets do not recommend that a bitch be sectioned more than three times in her lifetime.

If your bitch has labored unsuccessfully for some time and an emergency c-section is required, you may find that the outcome is not as positive as if the c-section was planned. The bitch is going into a major surgery exhausted. She may not have eaten or had fluids for several hours and may be dehydrated with her electrolytes out of balance. Placentas may have already separated from the uterine wall during the laboring process and there may be dead pups. The emergency c-section may well save the life of the remaining puppies but you do need to be aware that both mom and puppies are compromised when the surgery is done under emergency circumstances. If you are unable to see your regular vet for the emergency surgery, your bitch and puppies may be further compromised because emergency veterinary clinics do not see a lot of repro cases and are often not as skilled as you would wish. This is not a reflection on the skills and abilities of the emergency vet, but is simply a statement of fact. My experience has been that they simply do not move fast enough, and they do not listen to us.

Each vet will have preferences regarding the procedure of the actual surgery. Large dogs and small dogs may be handled differently simply because of the size and manageability issue. Discuss with your vets what their preferences are prior to the c-section if possible. Sometimes a vet will prefer to premedicate the bitch with a sedating drug such as valium prior to intubation while others will simply use a gas mask to put your bitch to sleep and then intubate her. Two of the safer gases used are Sevoflurane and Isofluorane. Your vet will have preferences, but you should take a pro-active role and ask in advance which gases will be used during the surgery. These two are highly desirable because they will leave the systems of the mother and babies more quickly.

The bitch must be intubated for two reasons. First, intubation will protect her airway and make sure that she is receiving oxygen during the surgery. Second, the gases used to anesthetize the bitch during the surgery will be passed by way of the intubation tube to the lungs. One thing is certain. It is necessary to utilize general anesthesia for a c-section on a bitch. Do not ask your vet about local anesthesia or epidurals for use on the canine patient. They must be kept quiet and still during the surgery and general anesthetic is the method used to accomplish that.

Once your girl has been anesthetized and intubated, she will be prepped for surgery. Her abdomen will be shaved, an IV will be started and she will be placed in a positioning tray on the surgical table. The surgeon and an assistant will scrub up, gown and glove prior to the surgery. You may be allowed to watch from the doorway, but usually your vet will want to maintain the sterile field and may not allow you to approach the surgical area. The surgical field will be draped with sterile paper drapes and you may not be able to see anything but the actual surgical site and the head of your bitch. Even if you are not allowed to watch the actual surgery, your services may well be needed to stimulate and rub puppies as they are delivered. If you know that you have a large litter, ask your vet if you need to bring along experienced people to assist in this process. Take a warming box with you.

The surgery will begin with an incision in the middle of the abdomen starting at the umbilicus and ending at the pubis. Once the surgeon has cut through the different layers of skin, underlying tissues and muscle, the uterus can be seen. The two uterine horns are then brought out of the body of the bitch. They will hang over her sides onto the drapes. The surgeon will then make an incision in the body of the uterus being very careful not to cut into the puppies inside. The goal will be to remove all of the puppies through the single incision, but in an emergency, other incisions may be made to quickly facilitate the removal of the puppies.

After the puppies have been removed from the uterine horns, they will be handed off to vet techs, the breeder and anyone else who can assist with the resuscitation of the puppies. The puppies will be under the influence of the anesthesia and will be lethargic. They will require vigorous rubbing, resuscitation and work. Vet techs who work with repro vets are wonderful in these situations and can be usually be trusted absolutely to know how to care 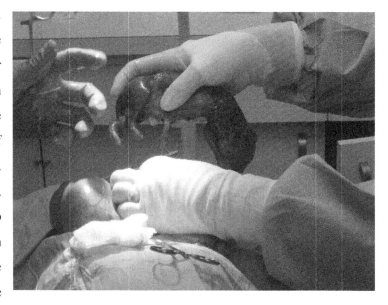 for your puppies. The umbilical cords will be trimmed, tied and swabbed with Betadyne® or another sterilizing agent. Once the puppies are well resuscitated, they will be weighed and tube fed to make sure that their glucose levels are appropriate.

As the puppies are being resuscitated, the surgeon will begin the closure of the wound. The uterine horns and any other abdominal structures that may have been contaminated with fetal fluids will be flushed with normal saline and placed back into the abdomen. The vet will close the wound in layers, with the interior layers being closed with suture material that will dissolve as the wound heals. The exterior stitches will require removal in 10-14 days. Don't confuse the removal of the stitches on the canine with what is done with a human c-section. A woman who has had a c-section can have her stitches removed in 3-5 days, and replaced with Steri Strips®. The center of gravity for the bitch is quite different because she walks on four legs with the entire weight of her abdomen on those stitches. Remember that the wound must be completely healed before the stitches can be removed. Your job during those 10-14 days is to watch the wound carefully for signs and symptoms of infection:

- Fever: Take a temperature each day for at least 10 days
- Redness at the wound site
- Warmth at the wound site
- Foul smelling discharge coming from the wound or vulva

Clean the surgical incision site daily with hydrogen peroxide and Q-tips or cotton balls. Check it carefully to make sure that hair and debris does not get into the wound area. Use clean tweezers to remove any debris that may be caught in the wound. Contact your vet if any of the signs above occur. Copious amounts of clear, pinkish or yellowish fluids seeping from the wound for days after the surgery is a sign that the wound is not healing and will require a vet's exam. If the wound is seeping large amounts of fluid AND you can easily hear the bowel sounds coming from the abdomen, the interior incision of the wound may have come apart. Call your vet and describe what you are seeing and hearing. Be specific. Try to describe exactly how much fluid is seeping from the wound. What color it is, how it smells, and how many little gauze pads are necessary to absorb the fluid are things the vet will need to hear. Remember, the wound should be dry and anything else should be reported to your vet.

Your bitch will usually be able to go home with you once she is fully recovered and has been given enough IV fluids to replace everything that might have been lost during the surgery. The vet will want to make sure that she is awake and that the puppies do not appear to be in distress before releasing her to go home with you. You can almost always take her home within a few hours following the surgery. Be very wary if your vet insists on keeping your bitch and her puppies at the vet hospital. Ask questions. Who will be there with her? What is the purpose of leaving her here? You know that you will be able to give her excellent care at home and unless there is a very good reason for her to spend the night in the vet hospital, do not allow her to do so. Once home, you may find that the bitch appears to be somewhat sleepy and dazed. She may not immediately begin to lick her puppies and she may not want to lie down and allow them to nurse. You may need to make a bed near her and stay with her for several hours in order to help her get settled with her babies. Full-term babies can usually nurse without assistance as long as you can keep the mom quiet and calm. She didn't have the advantage of the normal hormonal reactions to labor and delivery of the whelps that she would have had with a vaginal delivery, and she is still under the influence of the anesthesia. Stay with her and usually after a short period of time she will allow the puppies to nurse. After 12-24 hours, she will usually begin to assume her parenting duties without your support and assistance. The bitch will have often been given a pain medication at the vet's office and won't require anything to be given to her for pain once she is home. Remember that most pain meds will cross the barrier into the breast milk and your pups will receive it too, at a time when they need to be vigorously learning to nurse. Maiden bitches may take longer to come around than experienced moms, but most bitches will resume the normal care of the puppies within 24 hours.

If your vet does not send you home with an antibiotic for the mom, be sure to ask about it. It is generally accepted practice anytime following surgery in human medicine for antibiotics to be given as a prophylactic measure and can safely be given to a bitch following her c-section. Ask for it as a prophylactic measure. If you are giving an antibiotic to the mom, give it exactly as ordered and give mom a small amount of plain, live-culture yogurt each day that she is on the antibiotic. Put a small amount on your fingertip and give it to the pups as well each day that the mom is given the antibiotic. Antibiotics will often kill the "good" bacteria in the gut and the addition of even small amounts of live culture yogurt can replace the bacteria each day.

Following surgery, your girl may have a picky appetite for a day or so. Don't worry too much about it at this point. Feed her the foods that you know are her favorites and she will slowly begin to eat normally. A little pampering now won't create bad habits for later and mom deserves it.

Notes:

10- Removal of Dew Claws
They Aren't Opposable Thumbs

In some countries, the removal of dewclaws is forbidden, along with ear cropping and tail docking. There is a movement in many countries to show our dogs in their natural, unaltered state. In the US, these minor procedures are allowed. Dewclaw removal is considered a breeder's option in most breeds. If you wish to remove dewclaws, it is probably safer and less traumatic to mom and her babies for you to remove them yourself rather than take the puppies to the veterinary office where they might inadvertently be exposed to a disease process not present in your own home. Removal of dewclaws is a relatively simply process with minimal risk to the puppy as long as you follow some basic safety guidelines. Dewclaws are always found on the front paws and sometimes on the hind feet. The front dewclaw is located on the inside of the paw, roughly where a thumb is on the human hand. As the puppy grows, the dewclaw grows further up the leg until by adulthood, it is often more than an inch way from the other toes.

Dewclaws are visible on the back surface of the rear leg also about an inch or so above the foot. They do not appear to have a purpose. The dog does not seem to have muscle control in the dewclaw. They can be snagged on rough surfaces and have caused injuries to both front and rear feet. Because dewclaws do not serve an apparent purpose, their removal is a breeders' option in most breeds.

Newborn puppies do not have adequate clotting mechanisms until they are about 72 hours old. Time the removal of dew claws to occur between three and five days of age. Dewclaw removal on a five-day-old puppy using the technique that is discussed here is an almost bloodless procedure. Unfortunately, some breeds grow so quickly that by five days of age, the dewclaw has grown so large that removal is more difficult and possibly more painful for the puppy. Let your particular breed of dog and size of puppies be your guide in choosing to remove dewclaws on day three, four or five. Just remember that the younger they are, the more they will bleed because the clotting factors have not yet fully matured. Avoid removal of dewclaws prior to 72 hours old to prevent bleeding problems with your puppies.

Time to Remove Dew Claws

Use a warming box or a clean white towel on a counter top as your work surface. Be sure that the area is well lit. Have nearby, cotton balls or 4x4 gauze pads in case they are needed. In preparation for the dewclaw removal, wipe each dewclaw with Betadyne® solution or Hibiclens®. Allow this to dry completely. Do not use alcohol because it is an anticoagulant and will prolong bleeding if it occurs. Do not use hydrogen peroxide because it does not have adequate germicidal action. Depending on your puppies, you may need an assistant to hold the puppies.

You will need the following supplies:

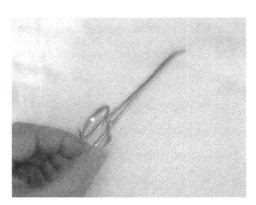

- Betadyne®
- 5 ½ inch long curved Kelly clamp with a locking mechanism (sometimes called a mosquito clamp— see picture at right).
- Super glue
- Permanganate of Potassium or styptic powder

Hold the puppy on to the warming surface in a comfortable position for him. Using the curved side of the Kelly clamp, work the curve of the clamp as far under the dewclaw as possible. The dewclaw should be well into the curve of the clamp, not at its tip end. Once the curved side is positioned well under the dewclaw, so that it can take as big a "bite" of the dew claw as possible, close it in one swift movement. It will close, lock and remove the dew claw all in one step. The edges of the cut skin will be held together neatly with the clamp. Using a fingernail, just scrape the nail off the clamp. Hold the clamp in place on the cut dewclaw for about 60 seconds before removing it. This

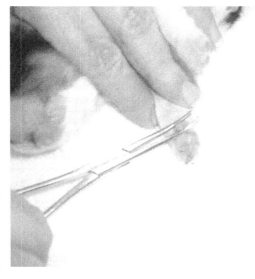

gives the blood time to clot. After 60 seconds, gently remove the clamp. Most of the time, you will see nothing there but a little straight line of fur that has been held together by the clamp. Drop two or three drops of Super Glue over the little straight line of fur and blow on it until the glue is dry.

If there is a drop or so of blood present when you have removed the clamp, use a 4x4 to apply pressure to the small sound before dropping the super glue drops onto the tissue. If bleeding continues use a pinch of Permanganate of Potassium or Styptic powder to the wound.

Dew Claws on the hind feet are sometimes a little trickier simply because of the positioning of the clamp against the flat surface of the leg. If the clamp feels awkward, simply use a pair of tweezers to pull the dewclaw away from the body and using a sharp pair of scissors, cut the dewclaw off. There is usually a bit more blood when you have used scissors because you don't have the advantage of the clamp holding the two cut ends together during the clotting time. Hold a sterile 4X4 to the area 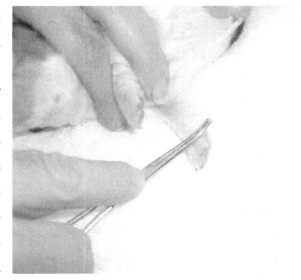 until the bleeding stops and then apply either the super glue, permanganate of potassium or Styptic powder to the wound. Watch the area for a day or so. The scabs and glue remnants will fall off in 7-10 days.

Notes:

11- I've Come to the End

Just in Case I Forgot: Puppies are Born 63 Days After Ovulation

I am sure there are things that I forgot to tell you, but over time as I remember them, I can add them in. My goal from the beginning was to write a book about canine reproduction and whelping using non-technical language and nonprofessional's language. I intentionally did not use many scientific words to describe the processes that I explained to you. We are not scientists; we are dog breeders. We think in breeding terms. Sure, I could have said copulatory lock every time I wanted to say, "tie", but it was not necessary. We all speak the same language; the language of love for dogs.

Most of us are here because we have had a negative experience with canine reproduction or whelping. We have had a missed litter, a dead litter, a sterile dog or bitch, or a terrified drive to the emergency clinic at 2 am. Worse yet, we lived so far away from help that we had to watch our puppies and sometimes even our bitch die. My purpose in writing this book was to give you the most current information I could find, put to rest some of the old breeder's myths that have been around for ages and correct some bad information that is quickly becoming new breeder's myths. I hope I have been able to do that. I wanted those of you who have never experienced a c-section to have all the information and education you need if you ever face one for your bitch; to understand the process. I wanted to introduce you to the three musketeers of whelping in a way that you would never forget. I hope that I have done that for you. That knowledge could will save a c-section some day in your future for a certainty.

I am positive that there are breeders out there who have fed a raw diet, supplemented with boat loads of calcium and never had a single c-section. Every bitch they owned ate their weight in calcium supplements every day and they delivered all 17 puppies within 10 minutes; no sweat. They will not believe the information that I have given to you. There are also people out there who smoked 4 packs a day for 60 years and never developed COPD or lung cancer too, but they are the exception, not the rule.

It was important to me that you understand why you must oversee the blood for progesterone levels once it is drawn from your girl. There were so many things that I hoped to accomplish and I do so hope that I have accomplished most of them. As usual, if you need me, I am reachable at myrasavant@hotmail.com . Please feel free to share with me your bad experiences and your good ones. I learn from each of you, collectively, far more than I could ever teach you.

Warming Box Ordering Form

You may order the regular warming box for **$175.00** and the deluxe warming box for **$225.00**. Both figures include shipping and handling within the continental United States.

The regular warming box contains:

- Plastic box
- Heating pad
- Bumpered pad
- Bulb syringe
- Tube feeding supplies
- Sub-cutaneous hydration supplies

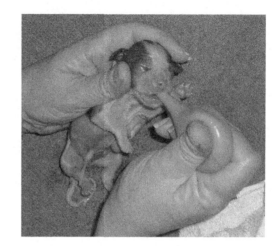

The deluxe warming box contains:

- The regular warming box
- Oxygen regulator
- Oxygen tubing

☐ Regular warming Box   ☐ Deluxe warming Box

Name	
Address	
City, State, Zip	
Phone Number	
E-Mail Address	

Send payment to:

Myra Savant-Harris

1561 Weathervane Ct

Fircrest, WA 98466

We accept check, money order or PayPal (e-mail address: myrasavant@hotmail.com)

Made in the USA
Las Vegas, NV
26 April 2024

89166918R00050